The Supreme Court and Its Publics

The Supreme Court and Its Publics

The Communication of Policy Decisions

Larry Charles Berkson
The University of Florida

Lexington Books
D.C. Heath and Company
Lexington, Massachusetts
Toronto

Library of Congress Cataloging in Publication Data

Berkson, Larry Charles.
    The Supreme Court and its Publics.

    Bibliography: p.
    1. United States. Supreme Court. 2. Publicity (Law)—United
States. I. Title.
KF8742.B44   347'.73'26   77-14793
ISBN 0-669-01994-1

Published simultaneously in Canada

Printed in the United States of America

International Standard Book Number: 0-669-01994-1

Library of Congress Catalog Card Number: 77-14793

To Sue

Contents

List of Tables

Preface

The evolution of this book has been rather lengthy. To properly acknowledge the many individuals who have contributed to its development, a brief history of the project is required. The project began during the winter of 1970 at the University of Wisconsin. A seminar codirected by Professors Joel Grossman and Stephen Wasby on the impact of the U.S. Supreme Court served as an initial stimulus. While searching for a research topic on the consequences of decisions, it became apparent that there was a large hiatus in the literature. Much had been written on compliance, noncompliance, evasion, and delay, but almost nothing existed on the process by which decisions were communicated to their targets. Consequently a research design of limited scope was developed. A questionnaire was prepared, and a number of small-town police chiefs were interviewed. The instrument was patterned largely after that utilized by Neal Milner in his study of four Wisconsin cities. The results were reviewed by each of the members enrolled in the seminar. Although their names are too numerous to recount here, Craig Harris, presently a budget analyst for the State of Wisconsin, deserves a special note of thanks for his insightful comments about the project. His and other critiques stimulated an expansion of the study.

Further investigation was temporarily interrupted, however, to allow time for the completion of a dissertation and several other projects. The study was renewed in 1973 after funding was obtained from the Division of Sponsored Research at the University of Florida. Especially helpful in this respect were Pat Rambo, Loretta Manning, and Diane Sherly. Monies were sufficient to undertake a large mail survey and to make site visits throughout the state. Insightful comments at this stage were offered by Eric Uslaner, now at the University of Maryland. Susan Carbon played a particularly important role in preparing, mailing, and coding the questionnaires. Mr. Brent Hampton was also helpful in this respect. Mr. Paul Cohen was of invaluable aid in facilitating the data analysis.

Several drafts of the manuscript were typed by Bonnie Earley and Susan Carbon. To them a special note of thanks is in order.

Professors David Fellman of the University of Wisconsin, Stephen Wasby of Southern Illinois University, Lawrence Baum of The Ohio State University, William Jenkins of Wayne State University, Lenore Haggard of the Center for Governmental Responsibility at the University of Florida, and Susan Carbon of the American Judicature Society read the manuscript in its entirety. Their insightful comments can hardly be underestimated. To them I am particularly grateful.

Finally, the many respondents to the questionnaires and those individuals who submitted to interview are extended a special note of appreciation for their kind cooperation. Obviously, without them the study could not have come to fruition.

The purpose of the study is to explore the communication of Supreme Court decisions to ten target groups in society. The major objective is to illustrate the applicability of communications theory in examining the process, rather than to draw finite conclusions about the impact of court decisions on the selected publics. Thus, the limitations of the data base are somewhat ameliorated. Nevertheless, it must be recognized that the survey sample is not random, as explained in Chapter 1, and the response rates are not ideal. Further, the data are confined to one state—Florida.

A section of Chapter 1 appeared in *Policy Studies Journal*, 2 (Summer 1974), 316-21. An altered version of Chapter 3 appeared under the title, "Supreme Court Justices: Effective Encoders of Supreme Court Decisions?" in the *American Business Law Journal*, 14 (Winter 1977), 391-404. Both are reprinted with permission.

1 Introduction

Ever since David Easton first introduced systems theory to political science, most policy analysts have utilized his five-fold scheme for studying the policymaking process: input, conversion, output, feedback, and environment.[1] Such diverse disciplines as international relations, public administration, comparative government, and domestic policy analysis have made use of the theoretical construct.[2] Generally, the conversion process has been overemphasized at the expense of other system components, most notably postconversion.[3] This is quite understandable; most political scientists perceive the "little black box" to be the key to understanding the authoritative allocation of goods and values to society. Easton himself neglected extensive study of the postconversion-prefeedback process. For instance in the first of his two books published in 1965, he devoted only two pages to output.[4] His model, moreover, almost exclusively emphasized the preconversion-conversion process. In all fairness, however, he did state that it would be vital to tract out the consequences of these outputs as they affect the environment and the system itself and create the types of conditions that nurture or destroy supportive sentiments.[5] Later the same year, he offered a more detailed analysis of the postconversion process.[6] For example, he established a typology of outputs: authoritative statements, authoritative performances, associated statements, and associated performances. Moreover, he distinguished between outputs and outcomes. "The actual decisions and implementing actions," he wrote, " are the outputs; the consequences traceable to them, however long the discernible chain of causation, are the outcomes."[7] Nevertheless, Easton still utilized his earlier schematic model emphasizing the preconversion-conversion process. He recognized the importance of outputs but generally in terms of feedback only: "they help to determine each succeeding round of inputs that finds its way into the political system."[8] In all, Easton devoted nineteen chapters to inputs (supports and demands) and only one to output.[9]

Gabriel A. Almond also has long been associated with a systems approach to studying political science. His position, and that of his colleagues, concerning outputs is made clear in one of his early publications. "It was the conviction of the colloborators in this study," he wrote, "that . . . the input functions, would be most important in characterizing non-western political systems, and in discriminating types and stages of political development among them."[10] In a later work he did establish a four-fold typology of outputs: extraction, regulation, allocation, and symbolic.[11] He did not, however, carry the analysis any further.

That same year, 1966, Thomas R. Dye used the systems model to explain policy outputs, which he calls outcomes, in American state politics.[12] The chief point of emphasis was again on conversion. He did not typologize outputs or even make the output-outcome distinction made the year before by Easton. Three years later, however, Ira Sharkansky, writing in essentially the same policy area, went a great deal further.[13] He distinguished between public policy, policy outputs, and policy impacts. "In brief," he wrote, "public policy represents actions taken by government; policy outputs represent the service levels which are affected by these actions; and policy impacts represent the effect the service has on a population."[14] In a later work on public administration, however, he did not use or elaborate on these distinctions. A typology of outputs was suggested in passing, but essentially the Eastonian emphasis, that outputs simply affect inputs, was followed.[15]

Despite the general lack of interest in postconversion aspects of systems theory, students of judicial politics have examined this area extensively. Indeed, for over a decade they have made a concerted effort to study the impact of U.S. Supreme Court decisions.[16] Martin Shapiro has noted that three distinct bodies of literature have evolved: studies on the impact of single Supreme Court decisions; studies on the impact of a series of Supreme Court decisions; and public opinion surveys.[17] The findings of each may be arranged in the conceptual model outlined in Table 1-1. Much work traditionally has been undertaken in the area of outputs. These are policies that are arrived at by the judicial policymaker or policymaking body. They may take the form of a directive, order, statute, decision, rule, or the like.[18]

Response to the policy may take at least four forms: compliance, noncompliance, evasion, and reversal seeking. Response is the immediate reaction of individuals and groups to whom the policy is directed. Do they comply overtly? In other words, have people changed their behavior?

Impact is often midrange. The question to be asked is not, did they comply overtly, but rather, did their compliance make any difference? Did the decision further the ideal toward which it was directed? More than a mere temporary behavioral change is involved. A social change is required.

Outgrowth is essentially an indirect impact. The question to be asked is, are there any side effects resulting from the policy, perhaps calculated or uncalculated? Again, the change is essentially social.

Finally, the long-range results may be analyzed in terms of outcome. In analyzing outcome one must ask, is the problem solved? An affirmative answer would indicate that a change in attitude, belief, culture, or philosophy has taken place.

Despite the development of at least modest theoretical underpinnings,[19] and the publication of a voluminous quantity of findings on the postconversion process, an important, if not crucial, component has often been neglected: the process by which policies are communicated to the public. This has been particularly true with students of judicial politics.[20]

Table 1-1
A Conceptual Model for Postconversion Analysis

	Output	Response	Impact	Outgrowth	Outcome
Description	Policy	Compliance Noncompliance Evasion Reversal seeking	Direct effects	Indirect effects	End result
Time Dimension		Immediate	Midrange	Midrange	Long term
Type of Change		Behavioral	Social	Social	Attitude Culture Philosophy Belief
Questions to be Asked		Do people comply?	Does the policy make any difference?	Are there any side effects?	Is the problem solved?

It seems premature to examine the response of the public or the impact, outgrowth, or outcome of a policy (decision) if there is no evidence that it is adequately communicated. A change in behavior, attitude, belief, or social structure can hardly be attributed to a particular decision if the individual (or society collectively) is unaware of the catalytic event. As Thomas Barth has stated: "Only after a policy-maker [in this case the recipient of a decision] has *perceived* Supreme Court decisions, can it be determined if his actions represent compliance, evasion or simple indifference."[21]

Communications research is hardly new. Several contemporary theories have been developed that contribute to those of the past.[22] For example, David K. Berlo has suggested that there are six ingredients in the process: source, encoder, message, channel, decoder, and receiver.[23] When person-to-person communication takes place, the source and the encoder may, at times, be grouped together, as can the receiver and decoder.

There are at least four factors within the source-encoder ingredient that can increase the fidelity of the message: communication skills, attitudes, knowledge level, and position within a social-cultural system.[24] First, communication skills include both writing and speaking, as well as thought or reasoning. Without clarity of thought, one's ability to encode is drastically impaired. Similarly without literary and linguistic faculties, a decoder, regardless of his brilliance, is unlikely to be able to understand the message.

Second, the attitudes of the source-encoder affect the ways in which he communicates. These include attitudes toward himself, the subject matter, and the receiver. For example if he lacks confidence in his message and is thus equivocal in his speech or writing, the decoder-receiver may discount the communique. Similarly if he has negative feelings about the message, this may be reflected in his presentation to the decoder-receiver. Finally, if the source-encoder favorably views the decoder-receiver, the communication will, in all likelihood, be more effective. As Berlo notes: "When readers or listeners realize that the writer or speaker likes them, they are much less critical of his messages, much more likely to accept what he says."[25]

Knowledge level is the third factor within the source that affects fidelity. It is obvious that the quantity of knowledge retained by the source-encoder about his subject will affect his message. A person simply cannot communicate something about which he either has no awareness or knowledge, or he does not clearly understand. Conversely, if the source-encoder is overly specialized, he may have difficulty in communicating the message in a nontechnical fashion so that the decoder-receiver may understand it.

Finally, the social-cultural system can affect the ways a source-encoder communicates. Whether or not he fulfills the general expectations of the social system will in part determine his credibility and thus affect his ability to communicate. If his beliefs and values "fit" with the dominant cultural mold, he is more likely to be effective. Moreover, his socioeconomic status within the system is important. If he is a member of certain groups rather than others, he may be a more effective communicator.

Berlo points out that there are three factors in the message that affect fidelity: the message code, the message content, and the message treatment. In the first place, the code must be comprehensible to the decoder-receiver. It must be written or spoken in an appropriate language and style, and appropriate vocabulary and syntax must be utilized. The content (substance) of the message must be arranged in a logical order and delivered (treated) in a sensitive fashion.

The channel in the communications process is the message vehicle. The choice of avenues is crucial and is determined by several factors, among which are: (1) those avenues available; (2) cost; (3) the encoder's preferences; (4) size and type of audience; (5) impact desired; and (6) length and style of the message. Obviously the choice of channels will affect directly the fidelity of the process. For example, if newspapers are selected and the intended audience is illiterate, the message will simply not be received.

The decoder-receiver, as suggested earlier, is the person at the terminal end of the communications process. He and the source-encoder are very similar. Indeed, the same four factors affecting the fidelity of the message within the source-encoder ingredient affect the decoder-receiver ingredient: communication skills, attitudes, knowledge level, and social-cultural system.

To summarize Berlo's theory of communication, an idea is communicated effectively only when each ingredient in the process is relatively free from interference.[26] Moreover, each ingredient is crucial to the process, and each may be affected by a number of factors. The process as a whole may be compared to a chain whose strength is only as great as its weakest link.

Perhaps more well known to political scientists is the "Two-Step Flow of

Communication" theory developed by Elihu Katz and Paul Lazarsfeld.[27] At one point it was assumed that a message was delivered directly from the source, through the channel, to the receiver. It was believed, for example, that the impact of editorials and articles printed in newspapers was direct. In other words, views were preceived as being formed directly by what people read. Katz and Lazarsfeld, however, refined this immature view of the communications process. Their research led them to conclude that "opinion leaders" often serve as intermediaries. These individuals are sought out by lesser informed members of society to supply them with information and value judgments. Moreover, it was also found that the opinion leaders themselves are influenced more by other "elites" than by the media.

The present study utilizes both the Katz-Lazarsfeld and the Berlo theories of communication to examine the process by which U.S. Supreme Court decisions are communicated to specific publics. Contemporary literature is utilized to evaluate the strength of the communications source (Supreme Court), the encoders (justices), and the message (decision). Additionally, a randomly selected sample of sixty constitutional law professors throughout the United States was asked to evaluate the writing skills of the twenty-one most recent justices.[28]

To assess the strength of the channels (media), the ability of the decoders (public elites), and the knowledge of the receivers (target publics), a six-page questionnaire[29] was mailed or delivered to ten selected publics in Florida: doctors, attorneys, judges, clergy members, school teachers, law enforcement officers, bookstore operators, moviehouse operators, school board members, and lawmakers. These occupations were chosen because they represent target groups of recent U.S. Supreme Court decisions. Obviously, the respondents investigated do not represent a random sample of the general population. Indeed, choosing them because of their occupational membership ensures that they are among the higher status elements of American society. Nearly 76 percent attended at least two years of college while 35 percent received graduate degrees. Five percent were Jewish, 14 percent Catholic, and 73 percent Protestant. Over one-half had occupied their positions in excess of six years.[30]

The survey instrument contained a combination of closed- and open-ended questions eliciting information about demographic variables, attitudes, perceptions, and levels of knowledge possessed by the respondents. The questionnaire was divided into two sections. The first requested general information and was administered to all the groups being studied. The second was devised especially for each individual group. Where possible a universe was surveyed. For example, questionnaires were mailed to every chief of police, sheriff, circuit judge, county judge, state attorney, public defender, state representative, state senator, and mayor. It was beyond the scope of this study, however, to survey the entire universe of some of the groups. In these situations an attempt was made to utilize random sampling techniques. This was possible in the cases of state troopers, private attorneys, assistant state attorneys, assistant public defenders, school board members, and county commissioners, because complete lists of members of these occupations were available. However, random sampling of city police officers, deputy sheriffs, doctors, bookstore operators, moviehouse operators, and school teachers was not possible. Police officers and deputies were surveyed in seventeen small- to average-size communities. Bookstore and moviehouse operators were selected from the yellow pages of Florida telephone directories. Clergy members were sampled in Miami, Gainesville, and Jacksonville. School teachers and doctors were surveyed in only one county, Alachua.

A cover letter accompanied each questionnaire. It explained the purpose of the study and named specific high-ranking officials who had approved of the project. Response rates varied from a high of 80 percent for state attorneys to a low of 12 percent for county commissioners.[31] Additionally, several interviews were conducted with members of each group.

The book is organized to parallel each of the six ingredients in the communications process. Chapter 2 contains a brief institutional history of the Supreme Court: its structure, politics, and major policy decisions. The purpose of this section is to acquaint the reader with the fluctuating attitudes about the Court. At its inception, it was not held in high regard. However, when John Marshall joined the ranks, its importance in the federal government increased tremendously. Its prestige was elevated simultaneously. During subsequent periods the reputation of the Court has vacillated from one of envy to one of uncertain skepticism. Subsequent to the historical discussion, a detailed evaluation is presented of the Court's legitimacy and prestige as well as the level of support it enjoys from the electorate. Such an analysis is crucial, for communications theory indicates that if the process is to be effective, the source must be perceived favorably in each of these respects.

Chapter 3 investigates the backgrounds, writing skills, status, and general reputations of the twenty-one Supreme Court justices prior to the ascent of Associate Justice Stevens. In this chapter, individual justices are evaluated and singled out for discussion. They are treated as encoders and are thus analytically distinct from the source—the institution itself.

Chapter 4 examines the language, style, timing, and mandates of Supreme Court opinions—the messages themselves. After determining that the justices actually write their own opinions, in contradistinction to other public officials, the quality of the prose, the clarity and conciseness of written opinions, as well as the quality of rationale utilized is discussed. Subsequently, attention is focused on the timing and mandate of the message.

Chapter 5 examines the various channels by which Supreme Court decisions are communicated to the public. Included is an evaluation of radio, television, newspapers, and periodicals (both general and specialized). The advantages and disadvantages of utilizing each conduit are examined. Data are presented on the media from which the various publics usually obtain reliable information about Supreme Court decisions.

In Chapter 6 the two-step flow of communication theory, cited earlier, is utilized to segregate message receivers into two distinct groups: the elites or intermediaries, and the ultimate receivers of Supreme Court decisions. Analytically, the former may be considered decoders and the latter receivers. The chapter focuses on three major categories of decoders: work-related personnel (bosses or superiors, coworkers, and subordinates); attorneys (public and private, as well as local judges); and miscellaneous individuals (instructors and friends). An in-depth look at law enforcement officers is undertaken. Data are presented about the decoders from whom they usually obtain reliable information about the Supreme Court. Data are also presented on their awareness and knowledge of Supreme Court decisions.

Chapter 7 investigates the quantity and quality of substantive knowledge retained by various occupational groups about the Court. These receivers were asked specific questions about Supreme Court decisions. Their responses are presented in tabular form. Only law enforcement officers, judges, and attorneys were accurate more than 50 percent of the time. Surprisingly, law enforcement officers ranked highest.

The final chapter presents a number of recommendations for reforming the entire process of disseminating Supreme Court edicts to target publics. An attempt is made to catalogue all the suggestions found in the literature as well as those that are suggested by the present research. They range from those that have a strong possibility of being adopted to those with little chance of success. Several suggestions are offered about ways in which the Court can maintain its high degree of legitimacy. Means by which the media may be facilitated, improved, and strengthened as conduits of messages are offered. Finally, suggestions are made about how to improve the quality of the opinions.

Notes

1. He first suggested using a political systems approach in *The Political System* (New York: Alfred A. Knopf, 1953), pp. 97-98. His first schematic model may be found in "An Approach to the Analysis of Political Systems," *World Politics,* 1957, 384.

2. Michael Brecher, et al., "A Framework for Research on Foreign Policy Behavior," *Journal of Conflict Resolution,* 13 (March 1969), 75-101; Ira Sharkansky, *Public Administration* (Chicago: Markham Publishing Co., 1970); Gabriel Almond and James B. Coleman (eds.), *The Politics of Developing Areas* (Princeton, N.J.: Princeton University Press, 1960); and Thomas R. Dye, *Politics, Economics and the Public Policy: Outcomes in the American States* (Chicago: Rand McNally, 1966).

3. For greater elaboration on this subject see Larry Berkson, "Post Conversion Analysis," *Policy Studies Journal,* 2 (Summer 1974), 316-21. Sections reprinted with permission.

4. *A Framework for Political Analysis* (Englewood Cliffs, N.J.: Prentice-Hall, Inc., 1965), pp. 127-28.

5. Ibid., p. 127.

6. *A Systems Analysis of Political Life* (New York: John Wiley and Sons, Inc., 1965).

7. Ibid., p. 352.

8. Ibid., p. 28.

9. Ibid., Chapter 22. He uses the term "output" in Chapters 27 and 28 but deals mainly with the feedback process.

10. Almond and Coleman, *supra* note 2, p. 17.

11. Gabriel Almond and G. Bingham Powell, *Comparative Politics: A Developmental Approach* (Boston: Little, Brown and Co., 1966), p. 27.

12. Dye, *supra* note 2.

13. The article, presented at the 1968 American Political Science Association Convention, Washington, D.C., may be found in Ira Sharkansky (ed.), *Policy Analysis in Political Science* (Chicago: Markham Publishing Co., 1970), pp. 61-79.

14. Ibid., p. 63.

15. Sharkansky, *supra* note 2, p. 7. "The outputs that administrators provide to their environment include services, tangible goods, and behavioral regulations, plus gestures, statements and activities which give messages to those who are tuned in."

16. For a summary of the most important material see Stephen Wasby, *The Impact of the United States Supreme Court* (Homewood, Ill.: Dorsey Press, 1970). For a collection of articles see Theodore Becker and Malcolm Feeley, *The Impact of Supreme Court Decisions* (New York: Oxford University Press, 1973).

17. Martin Shapiro, "The Impact of Supreme Court Decisions," *Journal of Legal Education*, 23 (1971), 77-89.

18. A number of scholars have suggested various typologies under which policies may be classified. See, e.g., Robert Salisbury and John Heinz, "A Theory of Policy Analysis and Some Preliminary Applications," in Sharkansky, *supra* note 13.

19. See, e.g., Stephen Wasby, "The Study of Supreme Court Impacts: A Roundup," *Policy Studies Journal*, 2 (Winter 1973), 138. But see Lawrence Baum, "An Organizational Theory of Judicial Impact," (Paper presented to the Midwest Political Science Association, 1973).

20. Stephen Wasby is one of the few scholars who has undertaken research in this area. See his *Small Town Police and the Supreme Court* (Lexington, Mass.: D.C. Heath and Co., 1976); "Communication of the Supreme Court's Criminal Procedure Decisions: A Preliminary Mapping," *Villanova Law Review*, 18 (June 1973), 1086-1118; "From Supreme Court to Policeman: A Partial Inventory of Materials," *Criminal Law Bulletin*, 8 (September 1972), 587-615; and "Getting the Message Across—Communicating Court Decisions to the Police,"

Justice System Journal, 1 (Winter 1974), 29-38. See also, Everette Dennis, "Another Look at Press Coverage of the Supreme Court," *Villanova Law Review,* 20 (March 1975), 765-99; David Grey, *The Supreme Court and the News Media* (Evanston, Ill.: Northwestern University Press, 1968); and Chester Newland, "Press Coverage of the United States Supreme Court," *Western Political Quarterly,* 17 (March 1964), 15-36.

21. Thomas Barth, "Perceptions and Acceptance of Supreme Court Decisions at the State and Local Level," *Journal of Public Law,* 17 (1968), 317 (emphasis added).

22. See, e.g., Franklin Fearing, "Toward a Psychological Theory of Human Communication," *Journal of Personality,* 22 (September 1953), 71-78; Claude Shannon and Warren Weaver, *The Mathematical Theory of Communication* (Chicago: University of Chicago Press, 1967); and Bruce Westley and Malcolm MacLean, "A Conceptual Model for Communications Research," *Journalism Quarterly,* 34 (Winter 1957), 31-38.

23. David K. Berlo, *The Process of Communication* (New York: Holt, Rinehart and Winston, 1960).

24. Fidelity is defined by Webster as "accuracy of reproduction." To Berlo, fidelity means that a source-encoder "will get what he wants. A high-fidelity encoder is one that expresses the meaning of the source perfectly." Ibid., p. 40.

25. Ibid., p. 47.

26. The technical term for interference in the communications literature is "noise." It is considered the opposite of fidelity. Ibid., pp. 40-41.

27. See Elihu Katz and Paul Lazarsfeld, *Personal Influence* (Glencoe, Ill.: The Free Press of Glencoe, 1955); and Elihu Katz, "The Two-Step Flow of Communication: An Up-to-Date Report of an Hypothesis," *Public Opinion Quarterly,* 21 (Spring 1957), 61-78.

28. Justice Stevens is excluded from this study because he was appointed during the course of the investigation.

29. The term "public," rather than "interest group" or "pressure group," is utilized to avoid the semantic argument over the exact definition of the latter phrases. For example, David Truman defines an interest group as experiencing a minimum amount of interaction between members of the group. It is the interaction that is "crucial" and "not the shared characteristics." Certain of the groups studied do not come within the definition. For purposes of the present study, a public is defined in terms of shared occupations. See David Truman, *The Governmental Process* (New York: Alfred A. Knopf, 1951), p. 24.

30. The above percentages represent adjusted frequencies.

31. See Appendix A for details.

2 The Communications Source: The Supreme Court

As suggested in Chapter 1, the source-encoder may be one and the same when interpersonal communication is taking place. However, the two are analytically separable when intercourse is less direct. The process presently under investigation falls into the latter category. The source is the Supreme Court, the institution itself: its roles, functions, and duties. Its efficacy is affected by society's perceptions of it. The encoders, on the other hand, are the specific individuals who comprise the Court. They have idiosyncratic characteristics, which have a separate but immediate and direct impact on the communications process. They are the subject of Chapter 3.

According to communications theory, the greater the legitimacy of the communications source, the greater the likelihood that the message will be accepted by its target public.[1] In other words, an institution held in great esteem and perceived as highly legitimate will be more efficacious than an institution viewed with skepticism. Thus, to determine the quality of the communications source, it is helpful, indeed imperative, to examine the position that the Supreme Court has occupied in the perceptions of society throughout its history.

A Brief History of the Court

The Supreme Court has occupied a vacillating posture in the minds of American citizens throughout the history of the United States. It is clear that the Court did not command a great deal of respect among many of the founding fathers. It had no cases to decide during the first three years of its existence, and a number of outstanding individuals, among them Patrick Henry and Alexander Hamilton, declined appointments to the bench. Its first chief justice, John Jay, resigned a short while after his appointment to become governor of New York. Associate Justice John Rutledge did not wait that long. Before the Court actually convened, he resigned to become chief justice of the South Carolina Supreme Court. Later Rutledge was nominated to be chief justice of the U. S. Supreme Court, but the Senate refused confirmation, whereupon Oliver Ellsworth assumed the position. Three years later Ellsworth "happily left office for a diplomatic post."[2] Another of President Washington's appointees, Robert Harrison, declined an associate position to become chancellor of Maryland. A fourth of the original six appointees, Thomas Johnson, resigned within a year of taking office. Nor was this trend confined to the Washington administration. John Jay again was appointed as chief justice, this time by President John Adams, but he declined the position. One of his reasons for refusing the appointment was that the Court lacked "energy, weight, and dignity."[3] Even Adams' greatest nominee, John Marshall, initially refused appointment to the Court.

With such a feeble beginning the Court's future was obviously in doubt. It was perceived as the weakest of the three branches of government and many believed it lacked potential for future development and growth. The Constitution had made only broad statements about its power and had limited its original jurisdiction to a relatively small number of cases. Control over the Court's appellate jurisdiction was placed in the hands of Congress. As Robert McCloskey has written, "neither the words of the Constitution nor the probable intent of those who framed and ratified it justified in 1790 any certitude about the scope or finality of the Court's power to superintend either the states or Congress."[4]

The uncertain position of the Court, however, was of brief duration. In perhaps one of the most momentous appointments in U. S. history, President Adams selected John Marshall, his secretary of state, to succeed Chief Justice Ellsworth. In the words of Henry Abraham, "it was Marshall who raised the Court from its lowly if not discredited position to a level of equality with the Executive and Legislative branches — perhaps even to one of dominance during the heyday of his Chief Justiceship."[5] There is little doubt about the accuracy of this assessment. Twenty-five years after the appointment, Adams told Marshall's son that his "gift of John Marshall to the people of the United States was the proudest act of . . . [his] life."[6] A recent poll of sixty-five experts on constitutional law unanimously ranked Marshall as "great," the only justice to receive such recognition.[7]

Scholars of the Court generally divide its history into various periods.[8] Uniformly, the first important analysis focuses on the Marshall era (1801–1835). Some of the Court's most momentous opinions were written by him. Indeed, the very foundation on which the judiciary rests today was established during his tenure. Perhaps his greatest opinion was *Marbury* v. *Madison.*[9] As Robert Cushman has written, "had the power of judicial review not been exercised and the doctrine established in the case of *Marbury* v. *Madison*, one may well conjecture whether our constitutional development would have been the same."[10] Indeed, most agree that it would not. Eighteen years later in a case of nearly equal import, the Court established its authority to review federal questions arising in state courts.[11]

Other great decisions involving state-federal relations were forthcoming. In *McCulloch* v. *Maryland*[12] the Court recognized the supremacy of national law to prevent states from attempting to destroy an agency of the federal government. Five years later the Court definitively established the supremacy of the national government in all matters affecting interstate commerce.[13] Another important opinion broadly interpreted the contract clause; the effect was to limit state legislative control over business corporations.[14]

On July 6, 1835, after almost thirty-five years of service on the bench,

Chief Justice Marshall passed away. President Jackson, deliberating for over six months, finally nominated Roger Brooke Taney as his replacement. Thus began the second era in the Court's history. Although a number of important decisions characterize Taney's tenure,[15] his Court is most remembered for its notorious *Dred Scott* decision.[16] Alienating an entire section of the nation, the opinion declared that native-born blacks could not become citizens. The direct effect was to nullify the Missouri Compromise of 1820 and lay the foundation for civil war. Even this "monumental aberration" could not destroy the Court's prestige and authority, although it did seriously impair the Court's impact on society for the next several decades.

During the post-Civil War period, seven chief justices came and went, each supporting to varying degrees the basic tenets of laissez-faire capitalism. Property rights were carefully guarded, and the "robber barons" were left relatively free to build vast economic empires. The income tax was held unconstitutional,[17] fostering the accumulation of vast sums by the wealthy elite. Judicial distinctions made between interstate commerce and manufacturing[18] and interstate commerce and mining[19] allowed industrialists maximum flexibility in expanding their monopolistic enterprises. In a number of other areas the Court was also highly supportive of the capitalists.[20] With the advent of the depression it stood steadfast against the new advocates of Keynesian economics,[21] and it was not until the famous "switch-in-time" that the Court altered its direction.

During this period, support for the institution was decidedly on the wane. It was vehemently attacked by Franklin Roosevelt and the New Dealers. The Court also stood relatively firm against extending fourteenth amendment privileges. In the *Slaughter-House Cases*[22] the majority strictly limited — and for all practical purposes destroyed—the privileges and immunities clause as a protector of individual civil liberties. Ten years later, by distinguishing between state and private action, the Court invalidated most of the Civil Rights Acts passed as appropriate legislation under the fourteenth amendment.[23] Subsequently the ill-fated *Plessy* v. *Ferguson*[24] decision was rendered, holding that state statutes requiring segregation of the races did not violate the Constitution.

On the other hand, the Court during this era did take the first steps toward incorporating elements of the Bill of Rights into the due process clause of the fourteenth amendment. In 1925, for example, freedom of speech was declared fundamental, thus limiting the states' ability to pass legislation restricting this aspect of a citizen's liberty.[25]

A fourth era in the history of the Court began with the decisions in *West Coast Hotel* v. *Parrish* and *National Labor Relations Board* v. *Jones and Laughlin Steel Corporation.*[26] In both cases Justices Roberts and Hughes switched their votes and held in favor of governmental regulation of the economy. It has been speculated that the reason for the change was in part due to the public's strong negative reaction against the Court's earlier decisions. Subsequently the Court has assumed that legislation in the economic sphere is constitutional unless it can be clearly proven otherwise.

However, the reverse became true for legislation affecting the basic freedoms of individuals.[27] The Court began slowly but increasingly incorporated most of the Bill of Rights and applied it to the states. With the appointment of Earl Warren as chief justice in 1953, the Court initiated a rapid expansion of the rights of defendants, minorities, and dissident groups. Such decisions as *Mapp* v. *Ohio,*[28] *Baker* v. *Carr,*[29] *Abington Township* v. *Schempp,*[30] *Miranda* v. *Arizona,*[31] *Katz* v. *United States,*[32] *Doe* v. *Bolton,*[33] and *Miller* v. *California,*[34] were particularly significant. Also during this era, one of the most important decisions in the Court's history was rendered.[35] In *Brown* v. *Board of Education* the Court finally declared that the "separate but equal" doctrine expressed in *Plessy* was "inherently unequal" and thus unconstitutional.[36] With this decision the Court laid the foundation for the greatest legal debate of the twentieth century, a debate that will likely remain unresolved for decades to come.

It is clear from this brief review that de Tocqueville's earlier observation on the power of the Supreme Court was most insightful.[37] Americans indeed have entrusted immense political power to their courts, and especially to the Supreme Court. Fred Rodell reaffirmed this sentiment over 120 years later when he wrote, "In no other nation on earth does a group of judges hold the sweeping political power—the privilege in practice, not just theory, of saying the last governmental word—that is held by the nine United States Supreme Court Justices."[38]

Whether the Court creatively fashioned this leading role in the political process[39] and whether such a role was envisioned for it by the founding fathers[40] is of little import today. The fact is that the Court has become the "Constitutional umpire" for the American political system. Indeed, in the words of the late Justice Frankfurter, "the Supreme Court is the Constitution."[41] As such, it has come to occupy a prominent, if not predominant, position in the American political process.[42]

This brief review also illustrates the fact that de Tocqueville's assessment of American society was correct: "Scarcely any political question arises in the United States that . . . is not resolved sooner or later, into a judicial question.[43] Because the Supreme Court is at the pinnacle of the legal system, its importance can hardly be overstated. In the words of Harold Laski, "the respect in which the federal courts, and above all, the Supreme Court are held is hardly surpassed by the influence they exert on the life of the United States."[44]

Perhaps because of the Court's tremendous authority and crucial role in the American political process, its activities have not always received universal approval. Congress has attempted, and on several occasions has actually curbed, the Court's activities.[45] Chief executives have likewise disapproved of some of its activities, and such notable presidents as Jefferson, Jackson, Lincoln, Franklin D. Roosevelt, and Nixon have been openly critical.[46] Moreover, at times the Court has fallen into general disfavor with certain segments of society.[47]

Finally, the Supreme Court has become a legitimate source of authority.

This is crucial, for as stated earlier, the greater the legitimacy of the communications source, the greater the likelihood that the message will be effectively communicated to its receivers.

Visibility as an Indicator of Legitimacy

There appears to be a consensus among scholars that the Court is not a highly visible institution.[48] It is suggested that the work of the Court is cloaked in secrecy and that little detailed information about it is possessed by the general population. For example, Krislov notes that *only* two-fifths of the adults questioned in a 1945 poll were cognizant of the number of Supreme Court justices.[49] Similarly, John Kessel has noted that more than one-fifth of his respondents in a Seattle survey were unable to articulate an opinion about the Court.[50] What is overlooked is the fact that there is a great deal of evidence to suggest that the Court is highly visible. If only two-fifths of the first poll did not know the correct number of Supreme Court justices, obviously three-fifths did. It would be interesting to determine what percentage of the population can state the correct number of congressmen or cabinet officers. Again, in the Kessel poll, if one-fifth of the respondents were unable to articulate an opinion about the Court, four-fifths or 80 percent were able to do so.

In other studies evidence is also found which suggests that the Court is highly visible. For example, as early as 1948 Gallup opinion polls found that only 17.3 percent of the respondents in one national survey and 13.6 percent in another, were unable to give the correct name of the highest court in the United States.[51] Thus, upon close scrutiny, the idea that the Court has little visibility is not as conclusive as many scholars would have us believe.

Another major problem with studies noted above is that they are predicated on the assumptions that, (1) the Court *should* direct its opinions to all 210 million people in the United States, and (2) that each citizen *should* be knowledgeable about every one of them. While it is true that nearly all decisions have at least some impact on each member of the populace, it is clear that each and every citizen need not be aware of all, or even most of, the Court's decisions. How many citizens need be aware of an antitrust decision, for example? Moreover, it is not necessary that all citizens be aware of cases having a broad impact on society. Is it imperative, for example, that the elderly be aware of the *Brown* decision? As a group, they will probably have little if anything to do with the educational system. On the other hand, it is far more important, indeed crucial, that members of various occupational groups be aware of specific decisions. What if the police and/or judges, for example, are unaware of *Miranda*? Obviously, if they are, important rights of citizens will be neglected.

Most Supreme Court decisions are directed toward a specific occupational group. For example, the defendants' rights opinions are aimed at judges, prosecutors, defense attorneys, and law enforcement personnel. Prayer and Bible reading opinions are directed at school board members and teachers. Obscenity opinions are directed toward bookstore and moviehouse operators. Other opinions likewise are directed toward specific receivers. Accordingly, in the present study there was no attempt to duplicate the work of public opinion polls and question a random sample of the general population about Court decisions. Indeed, as described in Chapter 1 the respondents represent the elite strata of society. Moreover, many of the awareness questions asked of the individuals in the survey are directly related to their occupations. Thus, one would expect the respondents to be much more knowledgeable about the Supreme Court and its decisions than the population in general.

To measure the visibility of the Court in the present study, two techniques were utilized. First, the respondents were asked general questions about the structure of the Court. These included questions about its size, the name of the chief justice, and the names of the associate justices. Second, the respondents were asked whether or not they were aware that the Court had rendered decisions in each of twenty-four decisionmaking areas.

Structural Visibility

Almost 76 percent (841) of the respondents correctly stated that there are nine justices on the United States Supreme Court. Only 14 percent gave an incorrect answer. Of these the most often cited number was seven, giving rise to speculation that these respondents were referring to the Florida Supreme Court, which is a seven-member body.

Nearly 74 percent of the respondents were able to name Warren Burger as the chief justice. Of the 107 (9.6 percent) who gave an incorrect answer, over half (59) stated that former Chief Justice Earl Warren held the position. A surprisingly large number of respondents were able to name several of the associate justices. Nearly 64 percent accurately named one or more, a majority were able to name between four and seven, and nearly 19 percent were able to name eight or nine.

General Awareness

Very little research has been undertaken on general public awareness about specific decisionmaking areas ruled on by the Court. A major exception is the work of Kenneth Dolbeare.[52] He asked Wisconsin respondents whether the Supreme Court had rendered decisions in each of eight subject areas. His findings are rather disappointing. The "Don't Know" rate equaled or exceeded the correct answer in five categories. In only two—prayers in public schools and segregation in public schools—did the rate of correct answers exceed 45 percent. Perhaps even more disheartening is the fact that only 2 percent of the 627 respondents were correct about all eight categories. Only 15 percent were correct about five or more of the areas, while 73 percent were correct about three or fewer areas. It is also important to note that in the three policy areas in which the Court had made no decisions (medicare, urban renewal, the John Birch Society), the number of incorrect answers was much higher than in all others. As Dolbeare suggests, this would seem to indicate "that there is a residuum of assumption that the Court has acted — or a willingness of respondents to say Yes to interviewers."[53] Thus, the number of correct answers in the remaining five areas is probably somewhat inflated. The extent to which this is true, however, remains an unanswered question.

Like the studies referred to earlier, Dolbeare utilized an empirically reliable cross-sectional sample of the general population. The limitations of this approach have been previously discussed. For purposes of the present study the Dolbeare technique was expanded to include twenty-four decisionmaking areas. It asked whether or not the U. S. Supreme Court had made a decision during the past twenty years in any of the areas listed. The findings are presented in Table 2-1.

A vast majority of the respondents stated that they were aware that the Court had issued opinions in the areas of right to counsel, obscene movies, death penalty, Lord's Prayer, Bible reading, and obscene books. In only two areas, drunk driving and birth control, was less than a majority of the respondents aware that the Court had issued pertinent opinions. Additionally, in only seven areas did the number of incorrect answers equal or exceed 10 percent. Perhaps most impressive is the fact that only 8.5 percent of the total number of responses were incorrect as compared to the 17.6 percent incorrect responses in the Dolbeare study.[54] As with that study, however, there is reason to believe that the "correct" percentages are somewhat inflated. In three control areas where the Court did not render decisions (flood damage, fire control, smoking), the percentage of incorrect answers was greater than in nearly all other areas. This would again indicate that at least some respondents venture opinions based on negligible or erroneous information or simply have a propensity to answer yes to these sorts of questions. Nonetheless, the fact that two of the areas elicited the greatest percentage of "unsure" responses indicates a basic honesty among the respondents.

Table 2-2 presents a breakdown of the responses by occupational group. As might be expected, attorneys and judges had a greater propensity to select correct answers than any other group. They were seldom incorrect and rarely selected the "unsure" response. Law enforcement officers rank a close third. At the other end of the spectrum, and again as might be expected, are arrayed moviehouse operators, school board members, clergy members, school teachers, doctors, and bookstore operators, respectively. They also most frequently chose the unsure response or were incorrect about the decisionmaking areas.

To further test levels of general awareness, the respondents were asked

Table 2-1
Awareness of Supreme Court Decisionmaking Areas[a]

Decisionmaking Areas	Percent Correct	Percent Incorrect	Percent Unsure
Flood Damage	16	25	51
Counsel	91	2	4
Obscene Movies	92	1	4
Juvenile Rights	83	2	11
Abortions	83	5	9
Drug Offenses	68	8	17
Wiretapping	93	1	3
Stop and Frisk	87	2	8
Fire Control	21	13	57
Vagrancy	63	10	20
Trial by Jury	76	8	12
Death Penalty	93	2	2
Lord's Prayer	93	2	2
Drunk Driving	27	34	31
Smoking	35	25	32
Bible Reading	90	3	5
Police Lineups	63	9	22
Reapportionment	71	5	19
Taxing Religious Orgs.	53	12	29
Birth Control	45	14	35
Double Jeopardy	60	9	24
Aid to Parochial Schools	68	6	21
Remain Silent	84	4	8
Obscene Books	89	3	5
Total Number	8270	2281	4778
Total Percent	69	9	18

[a]Percentages do not total 100 percent because of a few "no responses."

whether they were cognizant of two recent Supreme Court decisions directly affecting their occupational group.[55] Table 2-3 reports the findings. It is clear that the members of each group are much more aware of Court decisions directly affecting their occupations than they are of non-occupationally related decisions. This fact is readily discernable when comparing Table 2-3 with Table 2-2. Moreover, it is important to note that bookstore operators are much more aware of the ruling dealing with obscene literature than with obscene movies. Conversely, moviehouse operators are much more aware of the rulings on obscene movies than on obscene literature.

Surprisingly, doctors and clergy members were relatively unfamiliar with the birth control decision. Likewise, school teachers and school board members were relatively unfamiliar with the decisions involving aid to parochial schools. Law enforcement officers and lawmakers were relatively unfamiliar with the vagrancy ordinance decision. The low level of awareness about the birth control decision may be attributable to the fact that it is a rather old opinion (1965). On the

Table 2-2
Awareness of Twenty-four Decisionmaking Areas[a]

Occupational Group	Percent Correct	Percent Incorrect	Percent Unsure
Doctor (N = 1679)	62	11	28
Attorney (N = 2016)	80	4	13
Judge (N = 2760)	76	5	12
Clergy Member (N = 1488)	57	8	18
School Teacher (N = 2496)	62	11	22
Law Officer (N = 11926)	71	9	17
Bookstore Operator (N = 720)	63	9	25
Moviehouse Operator (N = 384)	54	15	29
School Board Member (N = 648)	57	11	27
Lawmaker (N = 2544)	67	9	18
Combined (N = 26,661	69	9	18

[a]Percentages do not total 100 percent because of a few "no responses."

other hand, the parochial school and vagrancy decisions are of rather recent vintage. In the latter case, very little media coverage accompanied the opinion and may partially account for the low levels of awareness. Such an explanation, however, clearly does not apply to the school aid cases. Indeed, as will be observed in Chapter 5, a number of specialized magazines carried critiques of the opinions, and newspapers have consistently carried feature stories on these decisions. Thus, the reason that school teachers and school board members are not generally aware of the school aid decisions remains a crucial but unanswered question.

Summary

The above analysis suggests a number of important points about the Supreme Court's visibility. First, the general public is not as unaware of the Court as an

Table 2-3
Awareness of Occupationally Relevant Supreme Court Decisions[a]

Occupational Group	Cases	Percent Yes	Percent No	Percent Unsure
Doctor (N = 70)	Birth control	56	26	16
	Abortion	90	1	6
Attorney (N = 84)	Seizure of evidence	93	4	4
	Right to counsel	93	5	2
Judge (N = 115)	Jury size	70	20	6
	Right to counsel	91	6	0
Clergy Member (N = 62)	Birth control	58	23	15
	Abortion	84	8	5
School Teacher (N = 104)	Aid to parochial schools	61	15	22
	School prayer	92	0	6
Law Officer (N = 497)	Seizure of evidence	80	12	6
	Vagrancy	61	27	11
Bookstore Operator (N = 30)	Obscene literature	73	10	17
	Obscene movies	53	20	23
Moviehouse Operator (N = 16)	Obscene literature	69	13	19
	Obscene movies	88	13	0
School Board Member (N = 27)	Aid to parochial schools	63	22	15
	School prayer	93	0	7
Lawmaker (N = 106)	Vagrancy	37	45	14
	Reapportionment	82	11	4

[a]Percentages do not total 100 percent because of a few "no responses."

institution as some scholars suggest. Large segments of society are able to articulate an opinion about it. Second, and as should be expected, elite members of society are much more aware of the Court and its decisions than is the general public. This is important, because they serve as decoders of Supreme Court messages (see Chapter 6). Third, if the Court's visibility is measured on a "need-to-know" basis, it is highly visible. Indeed, when asked about decisionmaking areas directly relevant to their occupations, respondents overwhelmingly claimed to be aware of them. Whether or not they have acquired substantive knowledge about the opinions, however, is another matter and is the subject of Chapter 7.

Support as an Indicator of Legitimacy

A second means by which to determine the legitimacy of the Court is to assess the degree of support (approval) for the institution. There are two readily distinguishable levels of support: specific and diffuse.[56] Specific support is the extent to which the public praises or criticizes particular decisions of the Supreme Court. Several studies have attempted to make such an assessment with varying results. For example, a Harris survey in November 1966 revealed that 76 percent of the sample favored decisions on reapportionment and that 64 percent favored desegregation of schools and public accommodations.[57] The sample was almost evenly split on the rulings denying passports to communists and decidedly disfavored the *Miranda* (65 percent) and School Prayer decisions (70 percent). A subsequent poll by the Gallup organization reported that 58 percent of their respondents favored the Court's obscenity rulings. However, 57 percent disapproved of the death penalty and the newsman's confidential sources cases. Similarly, 53 percent opposed the Court's parochial school aid decisions.[58] Overall, it appears that the Court received little specific support during Chief Justice Warren's latter years.[59] Thus, as Murphy and Tanenhaus have suggested, "specific support of the Supreme Court is . . . very heavily policy determined."[60]

The second level of support, diffuse support, is perhaps more important in assessing the Court's legitimacy, for as Krislov has written, "Public response . . . is not dependent upon interpretation of any single case, no matter how momentous. Rather, it is derived from the total impression made by the Court upon large numbers of people."[61] A superficial examination of the extant literature might lead one to conclude that the Court is held in relatively low esteem. For example, in his 1966 study of public opinion in Wisconsin, Kenneth Dolbeare found that the Supreme Court was perceived as least important of the three branches of national government. It was ranked lowest in terms of public confidence in actions taken by it, and it received a "very good" rating from only 8 percent of the sample.[62] However, a more careful analysis suggests that the Court is regarded fairly well. First, in his own study Dolbeare found that only 6 percent of his respondents rated the Court's performance as poor. Similarly, in a 1967 Gallup poll, only 17 percent of the respondents rated the Court in this manner.[63] Further, John Kessel found that only 26 percent of his respondents in Seattle held critical attitudes about the Court.[64]

Second, it should be noted that the above surveys were conducted at a time when the Court was under strong attack by conservative as well as moderate elements in American society. As such, one would expect these figures to underrepresent "usual" support for the Court. Indeed, survey data indicate this to be true. According to a 1949 Gallup poll, 60 percent of the respondents in a national survey rated the Court as excellent or good. By 1967, at the height of the Warren Court activism, the rating had fallen to 45 percent. Two years later it was down to 33 percent.[65] However, by 1973 the rating had risen to 37 percent.

Apparently the upward trend is continuing. According to a Harris survey of 1971, only 23 percent of the respondents stated they had a great deal of confidence in the Court, but by 1974, 40 percent of those surveyed responded positively to the same question.[66]

Third, as Goldman and Jahnige have observed, "a widespread lack of popular support for a specific set of judges should not be taken as indicative of a lack of support for the Court as an independent institution."[67] Most research fails to take this distinction into account. Of course, scholars and pollsters are not the only groups to make this error. President Franklin D. Roosevelt apparently did so in 1937. The result was an abortive court-packing plan. The vehement resistance that followed is simply another indication of the widespread inherent support for the Court as an institution.

Fourth, it is suggested that drawing conclusions from empirical research alone is too narrow an approach. Even if one overcomes problems of sampling, there remain serious methodological problems in determining the reliability of a respondent's answer. Moreover, the statistical data tell us little, if anything, about the intensity with which the public supports or rejects the Court as a decision-making body. Thus, it is helpful and important to examine the work of normative theorists in this area.

Perhaps the most well reasoned critique, and one which typifies the classic literature on the subject, was written shortly after a period of extremely intense anti-Court feeling.[68] Noting that the Court had survived a number of "real" and "dangerous" attacks, Max Lerner asked rhetorically, "what accounts for the extraordinary toughness and viability of the Court?"[69] His answer is clear: "Its survival thus far shows that it has deep historical and psychological roots in American life . . . it has a strong symbolic hold over the American mind."[70] Thus, "support of the judicial power lies largely in the psychological realm; its roots are in the minds of the people."[71]

To Lerner, the "Supreme Court as a symbol goes hand in hand with the Constitution as a symbol."[72] The importance of this idea cannot be overestimated, for as he writes, "Every tribe needs its totem and its fetish, and the Constitution is ours."[73] Indeed, he persuasively argues that some day when a "real" religious history of America is written it will be about "the worship of the Constitution and the Supreme Court."[74] He views "the cult of the Supreme Court" as the "emotional cement by which American capitalism and democracy are held together."[75] In other words, the Court has become a "symbol" of justice to the public, and although it may occasionally be attacked, its decisions are generally perceived as legitimate and authoritative. Thus, as Professor Schmidhauser has concluded, "while it is true that public attitudes reflecting the Court fluctuate, a residuum of deference if not reverence remains one of the sources of psychic income for the justices."[76]

In the present study respondents were asked whether they believed the Supreme Court is an important part of the national government. They were also asked whether they thought that it is important to be aware of its decisions and whether the decisions affected their personal lives and occupations. It is clear from Table 2-4 that the respondents to the survey perceive the Court as important. Apparently they also believe its decisions affect both their familial and occupational lives. Finally the respondents believe that it is important to be aware of the Court's decisions.

Compliance as an Indicator of Legitimacy

A third means by which to assess the legitimacy of the Court is to determine whether there is compliance with its decisions. Michael Petrick has suggested that legitimacy is not synonymous with "approval" or "rightness."[77] Rather, legitimacy is "the process by which authority is accepted."[78] Utilizing such a definition, it is possible that individuals may highly disapprove of certain decisions but not challenge the Court's basic authority to issue them. The distinction between approval and acceptance (legitimacy) becomes particularly apparent during periods when the Court is extremely unpopular. For example, it is clear that the Court did not reflect public sentiment when it declared much of the New Deal legislation unconstitutional. However, attempts to "pack the Court" to effect a change were met with strong opposition, much of it from some of the Court's most vehement critics.

Full compliance, of course, is rarely, if ever, achieved.[79] But the existence of noncompliance does not necessarily indicate a lack of legitimacy. Rather, it

Table 2-4
Perceptions of the U. S. Supreme Court[a]

	Yes	No	Unsure
Do you feel that the U. S. Supreme Court is an important part of our national government?	1036 (93.2%)	33 (3.0%)	39 (3.5%)
Do you feel it is important to be aware of decisions of the U. S. Supreme Court?	1093 (98.4%)	3 (.3%)	13 (1.2%)
Do the decisions of the U. S. Supreme Court affect your personal life (family and freedom)?	1053 (94.8%)	36 (3.2%)	20 (1.8%)
Do the decisions of the U. S. Supreme Court affect your work?	1077 (96.9%)	21 (1.9%)	13 (1.2%)

[a]Percentages do not total 100 percent because of a few "no responses."

may reflect a means by which the public temporarily voices its opposition to a decision. As Petrick has stated, "compliance . . . need not be immediate and complete. Such things as promises to comply, and token compliance, can and do indicate some degree of legitimation of a Court action."[80] For example, almost no integration took place for years after the *Brown* decisions of 1954 and 1955.[81] Gradually, however, integration did occur. Furthermore, nowhere in the voluminous quantity of literature on compliance and noncompliance with Supreme Court decisions is it reported that the general population has successfully resisted an edict by the Court for any substantial length of time.

Conclusions

Whether one utilizes visibility, support (approval), or compliance as indicators of legitimacy, it can be effectively argued that the Supreme Court is a respected and highly legitimate source of authority.[82] As an institution it appears to be deeply entrenched in the political system. Even when the electorate appears to be displeased with its decisions, there is a general unwillingness to impeach one of its members or tamper with its size or jurisdiction. Indeed, as David Lawrence has concluded, the American people "have accepted the doctrine that it is fundamentally unethical to refuse to respect an adverse decision" of the U. S. Supreme Court.[83]

Notes

1. See, e.g., David Berlo, *The Process of Communication* (New York: Holt, Rinehart and Winston, 1960), p. 41; Nan Lin, *The Study of Human Communication* (New York: Bobbs-Merrill Co., 1973), pp. 106-108. See especially David Bell, *Power, Influence and Authority* (New York: Oxford University Press, 1975), pp. 26-30; C. I. Hooland and Walter Weiss, "The Influence of Source Credibility Effectiveness," *Public Opinion Quarterly,* 15 (Winter 1951), pp. 635-650; and C. I. Hooland, "Reconciling Conflicting Results Derived from Experimental and Survey Studies of Attitude Change," *American Psychologist,* 14 (1959), 8-17.

2. Henry Abraham, *The Judicial Process* (New York: Oxford University Press, 1968), p. 345.

3. Henry Abraham, *Justices and Presidents* (New York: Oxford University Press, 1974), p. 73.

4. Robert McCloskey, *The American Supreme Court* (Chicago: University of Chicago Press, 1967), p. 9.

5. Abraham, *supra* note 3, p. 75.

6. Quoted in Charles Warren, *The Supreme Court in United States History* (Boston: Little, Brown and Co., 1928), vol. 1, p. 178.

7. Albert Blaustein and Roy Mersky, "Rating Supreme Court Justices," *American Bar Association Journal,* 58 (November 1972), 1183-1187.

8. See, e.g., Edward Corwin, *The Twilight of the Supreme Court* (New Haven, Conn.: Yale University Press, 1935), pp. 180-182; C. Herman Pritchett, *The American Constitution* (New York: McGraw-Hill Book Co., 1968), pp. 51-58; and Rocco Tresolini, *American Constitutional Law* (New York: Macmillan Co., 1965), pp. 15-25.

9. 1 Cranch 137, 2 L.Ed. 60 (1803).

10. Robert Cushman, *Cases in Constitutional Law* (Englewood Cliffs, N.J.: Prentice-Hall, 1975), p. 11.

11. Cohens v. Virginia, 6 Wheaton 264, 5 L.Ed. 579 (1821).

12. 4 Wheaton 316, 4 L.Ed. 579 (1819).

13. Gibbons v. Ogden, 9 Wheaton 1, 6 L.Ed. 23 (1824).

14. Dartmouth College v. Woodward, 4 Wheaton 518, 4 L.Ed. 629 (1819).

15. See, e.g., Cooley v. Board of Wardens, 12 Howard 299, 13 L.Ed. 996 (1851); and Charles River Bridge v. Warren Bridge, 11 Peters 420, 9 L.Ed. 773 (1837).

16. Dred Scott v. Sanford, 19 Howard 393, 15 L.Ed. 691 (1857). Henry Abraham has written, "it is a pity that Taney is so often remembered by that case rather than by his supreme accomplishments in achieving governmental concord and constitutional understanding." Abraham, *supra* note 3, p. 92.

17. Pollock v. Farmer's Loan and Trust Co., 158 U. S. 601 (1895).

18. United States v. E. C. Knight, 156 U. S. 1 (1895); and Hammer v. Dagenhart, 247 U. S. 251 (1918).

19. Oliver Iron Mining Co. v. Lord, 262 U. S. 172 (1923).

20. See, e.g., Bailey v. Drexel Furniture Co., 259 U. S. 20 (1922); and Lochner v. New York, 198 U. S. 45 (1905).

21. See, e.g., Schechter Poultry Corporation v. United States, 294 U. S. 495 (1935); Carter v. Carter Coal Co., 298 U. S. 238 (1936); and United States v. Butler, 297 U. S. 1 (1936).

22. 16 Wallace 36, 21 L.Ed..394 (1873).

23. Civil Rights Cases, 109 U. S. 3 (1883).

24. 163 U. S. 537 (1896).

25. Gitlow v. New York, 268 U. S. 652 (1925).

26. 300 U. S. 379 (1937); and 301 U. S. 1 (1937), respectively.

27. For a remarkably enlightening account of this "double-standard," see Henry Abraham, *Freedom and the Court* (New York: Oxford University Press, 1972), Chapter 2.

28. 367 U. S. 643 (1961).

29. 369 U. S. 186 (1962).

30. 374 U. S. 203 (1963). See also companion case, Murray v. Curlett, ibid.

31. 384 U. S. 436 (1966).

32. 389 U. S. 347 (1967).

33. 410 U. S. 179 (1973). See also Roe v. Wade, 410 U. S. 113 (1973).

34. 413 U. S. 15 (1973). See also Paris Adult Theater v. Slaton, 413 U. S. 49 (1973).

35. It is generally ranked in importance with *Marbury* v. *Madison*, 1 Cranch 137, 2 L.Ed. 60 (1803) and *Dred Scott* v. *Sanford*, 19 Howard 393, 15 L.Ed. 691 (1857).

36. Brown v. Board of Education, 347 U. S. 483 (1954).

37. Alexis de Tocqueville, *Democracy in America* (New York: Washington Square Press, 1964), p. 50.

38. Fred Rodell, *Nine Men* (New York: Vintage Books, 1955), p. 33.

39. Mary Walker, *The Evolution of the United States Supreme Court* (Morristown, N.J.: General Learning Press, 1974), p. 3.

40. Ibid., p. 10.

41. Rodell, *supra* note 38, p. 34.

42. Stephen Wasby, *American Government and Politics* (New York: Charles Scribner's Sons, 1973), p. 578.

43. Alexis de Tocqueville, *Democracy in America* (New York: Alfred A. Knopf, 1946), vol. I, p. 280.

44. Harold Laski, *The American Democracy* (New York: Viking Press, 1948), p. 110.

45. See, e.g., Walter Murphy, *Congress and the Court* (Chicago: University of Chicago Press, 1962), pp. 127-241; Stuart Nagel, "Court-Curbing Periods in American History," *Vanderbilt Law Review,* 18 (June 1965), 925-944; and C. Herman Pritchett, *Congress Versus the Court* (Minneapolis: University of Minnesota Press, 1961).

46. See, e.g., Robert Jackson, *The Struggle for Judicial Supremacy: A Study of a Crisis in American Power Politics* (New York: Alfred A. Knopf, 1941); and Robert Scigliano, *The Supreme Court and the Presidency* (New York: The Free Press, 1971).

47. Robert McCloskey has noted "that the Court has seldom strayed very far from the mainstream of American life and seldom overestimated its own power and resources." McCloskey, *supra* note 4, p. 225. This conclusion permeates the literature on the Supreme Court. See, e.g., W. W. Willoughby, *The Supreme Court of the United States* (Baltimore: Johns Hopkins Press, 1890), p. 114; and Alexander Bickel, *The Supreme Court and the Idea of Progress* (New York: Harper and Row, Inc., 1970), pp. 94-95.

48. See, e.g., Walter Murphy and Joseph Tanenhaus, "Public Opinion and the United States Supreme Court," in Joel Grossman and Joseph Tanenhaus (eds.), *Frontiers of Judicial Research* (New York: John Wiley and Sons, 1969), pp. 276-280.

49. Samuel Krislov, *The Supreme Court in the Political Process* (New York: The Macmillan Co., 1965), p. 152.

50. John Kessel, "Public Perceptions of the Supreme Court," in Theodore Becker and Malcolm Feeley (eds.), *The Impact of Supreme Court Decisions* (New York: Oxford University Press, 1973), p. 191.

51. Walter Murphy and Joseph Tanenhaus, "Public Opinion and the United States Supreme Court," *Law and Society Review,* 2 (May 1968), 361, note 5.

52. Kenneth Dolbeare, "The Public Views the Supreme Court," in Herbert Jacob (ed.), *Law, Politics, and the Federal Courts* (Boston: Little, Brown and Co., 1967), pp. 194-212.

53. Ibid., p. 199.

54. Incorrect responses in the Dolbeare study were computed from Table 4. Ibid., p. 200.

55. They were not asked about the case by name, although in some instances it was supplied.

56. See Murphy and Tanenhaus, *supra* note 48, pp. 286-294.

57. Stephen Wasby, *The Impact of the United States Supreme Court* (Homewood, Ill.: Dorsey Press, 1970), p. 238.

58. Stephen Wasby, *Continuity and Change: From the Warren Court to the Burger Court* (Pacific Palisades, Cal.: Goodyear Publishing Co., 1976), pp. 80-81.

59. Sheldon Goldman and Thomas Jahnige, *The Federal Courts as a Political System* (New York: Harper and Row, 1971), p. 135.

60. Murphy and Tanenhaus, *supra* note 51, at 373.

61. Krislov, *supra* note 49, p. 153.

62. Dolbeare, *supra* note 52, p. 203.

63. See Wasby, *supra* note 57.

64. Kessel, *supra* note 50, p. 195. The percentage was derived by calculations performed on the table.

65. Reported in Goldman and Jahnige, *supra* note 59, p. 135, note 70.

66. Reported in Wasby, *supra* note 58, pp. 80-81.

67. Goldman and Jahnige, *supra* note 59, pp. 145-146.

68. Max Lerner, "Constitution and Court as Symbols," *Yale Law Journal,* 46 (June 1937), 1290-1319.

69. Ibid., at 1291.

70. Ibid., at 1292.

71. Ibid.

72. Ibid., at 1293.

73. Ibid., at 1294.

74. Ibid., at 1295. But see Walter Murphy, Joseph Tanenhaus, and Daniel Kastner, "Public Evaluations of Constitutional Courts: Alternative Explanations," *Sage Professional Papers in Comparative Politics,* 1, 01-001 (Beverly Hills, Cal. and London: Sage Publications, 1973), p. 13.

75. Lerner, *supra* note 68, at 1306. See also Jerome Frank, *Courts On Trial* Princeton, N.J.: Princeton University Press, 1973), Chapter 18.

76. John Schmidhauser, "The Justices of the Supreme Court: A Collective Portrait," *Midwest Journal of Political Science,* 3 (February 1959), 4.

77. Michael Petrick, "The Supreme Court and Authority Acceptance," *Western Political Quarterly,* 21 (March 1968), 5-19.

78. Robert Presthus, "Authority in Organizations," *Public Administration Review*, 20 (Spring 1960), 87.

79. See, e.g., Wasby, *supra* note 57, Chapter 2.

80. Petrick, *supra* note 77, at 8.

81. Brown v. Board of Education, 347 U. S. 483 (1954); 349 U. S. 294 (1955).

82. For an excellent discussion of the Court's source of authority see Petrick, *supra* note 77.

83. Quoted in William Barnes and A. W. Littlefield, *The Supreme Court Issue and the Constitution* (New York: De Pamphilis Press, 1937), p. 51. See also William Daniels, "The Supreme Court and its Publics," *Albany Law Review,* 37 (July 1973), 632, 638-639; and Arthur Miller, "Some Pervasive Myths About the United States Supreme Court," *St. Louis University Law Journal,* 10 (Fall 1965), 153.

3 The Encoders: Supreme Court Justices

The second ingredient in the communications network is the encoders—the Supreme Court justices themselves. Prior to discussing this ingredient, however, it must be determined that the justices themselves actually write the decisions. If they do not, of course, it might be argued that an important link in the communications process is missing. Indeed, it would be meaningless to analyze the justices' communications skills if the messages are not the products of their own hand.

Some scholars have suggested that law clerks play a substantial role in writing opinions. It is true that clerks perform a wide variety of tasks. Moreover, it is known that some are given an opportunity to draft an occasional opinion. However, it is generally believed that by the time a justice finishes editing the opinion, a clerk may very well not recognize his own work.[1] The major exception appears to have been the drafts written by the clerks of Chief Justice Vinson. Jerome Frank, a former clerk to Justice Black, relates the "rumor" that Vinson did "all his 'writing' with his hands in his pockets, outlining to his clerks generally what he wanted and then criticizing this bit or that in a clerk's draft and making suggestions for revision."[2] Nonetheless, such speculations are rare, and the overwhelming consensus among scholars of the Court is that, unlike officials in the executive and legislative branches of government who regularly employ ghost writers, the vast majority of justices jealously guard the prerogative of writing their own opinions.[3] With the prefatory remarks in mind, we now move to an analysis of the Supreme Court encoders.

Communications theory suggests that an effective encoder must (1) occupy a respected position in society, (2) be highly educated and well-informed, and (3) possess requisite communications skills.

The Status of Supreme Court Justices

There is little doubt that Supreme Court justices occupy a position of extremely high prestige in this country. As notable scholars have concluded, "on occupational and social continuums, they rank in the top position."[4] Although many studies investigating occupational status fail to include the category, "Justice of the United States Supreme Court,"[5] some have done so. For example, as early as 1943, Mapheus Smith found that Supreme Court justices ranked highest on an empirical scale of prestige status occupations.[6] The first extensive study was

29

undertaken in 1947 by the National Opinion Research Center.[7] Respondents
were asked to evaluate each of ninety occupations as having either excellent,
good, average, somewhat below average, or poor standing in society. Overall,
the status of U. S. Supreme Court justice ranked highest. Of the respondents,
83 percent gave the occupation an excellent rating, 15 percent a good rating,
and only 2 percent an average rating. None gave it below average or poor
ratings. In 1963, a group of scholars replicated the study to determine shifts
in perceptions.[8] Again, the position of Supreme Court justice ranked first
with no substantial change in specific ratings.

The Education and Backgrounds of Supreme Court Justices

It has long been recognized that Supreme Court justices generally come from
backgrounds which suggest that they are highly educated and well-informed.[9]
According to Professor Schmidhauser, between 1789-1959, 91 percent of the
justices came from economically comfortable surroundings and socially pres-
tigious and politically influential families.[10] Over one-third were related to
former jurists and were intimately connected with families possessing a tradition
of judicial service.[11] During that same period, approximately one-third of the
justices acquired an undergraduate and/or graduate education at one of the
reputable Ivy League schools.[12] Between 1933-1957, 61 percent of the justices
attended undergraduate colleges or universities of high standing, while 62 percent
attended law schools of high standing.[13]
    Between Chief Justice Warren's ascent to the bench in 1953 and the retire-
ment of Justice Douglas, twenty-one justices held a seat on the Court. The vast
majority held solid credentials upon appointment and served with dedication,
intelligence, and judicial excellence. Table 3-1 summarizes the most important
aspects of the justices' backgrounds. It is interesting to note that only Justices
Black, Harlan, Jackson, Marshall, and Burger do not hold degrees from pres-
tigious law schools. Equally interesting is the fact that while most of the justices
have had a great deal of prior legal experience before ascending the bench, most
have had relatively limited experience as judges. Only Justices Minton, Burger,
and Blackmun had eight or more years of such service before joining the Court.
On the other hand, as Professor Abraham has observed, "many of the most
illustrious men in the history of the Court were judicially inexperienced."[14] He
points out that by late 1973, only twenty-two justices had had ten or more
years experience on any tribunal—federal or state—and forty-two had had no
judicial experience at all. Several justices have had extensive nonjudicial experience. Many have been law school professors, members of Congress, or
members of the executive branch of government.
    Table 3-2 reports the findings of two separate studies. The first was under-
taken by Professors Albert Blaustein and Roy Mersky.[15] Sixty-five law school

Table 3-1
Background of the Twenty-one Most Recent Justices[a]

Justice	Appointed	Undergraduate Education	Graduate Education	Prior Legal Positions Held	Other Positions Held
Warren	Eisenhower–1953	University of California	University of California	Attorney General of California (4)[b]; District Attorney in California (14)	Governor of California (10)
Black	Roosevelt–1937	Ashland College	Alabama	Police Court Judge, Alabama (1); County Solicitor	U. S. Senate (10)
Reed	Roosevelt–1938	Kentucky Wesleyan Yale	Columbia Virginia	Solicitor General (3) Government Counsel (6)	Chairman President's Com. on Civil Service Improvement
Frankfurter	Roosevelt–1939	City College of New York	Harvard	Assistant United States Attorney (4)	Assistant to War Secretary (1) Professor, Harvard (25)
Douglas	Roosevelt–1939	Whitman College	Columbia		Chairman, Securities and Exchange Commission (3); Dean, Yale Law School
Jackson	Roosevelt–1941		Albany Law School	Attorney General (1) Solicitor General (2)	
Burton	Truman–1945	Bowdoin College	Harvard	Director of Law, City of Cleveland (3)	Mayor of Cleveland (5); U. S. Senate (4)
Clark	Truman–1949	University of Texas	Texas	Attorney General (4) Dallas County District Attorney (5)	
Minton	Truman–1949	Indiana	Indiana Yale	U. S. Court of Appeals (8)	U. S. Senate (6)
Harlan	Eisenhower–1955	Princeton	New York Law School	U. S. Court of Appeals (1)	New York State Crime Commission (2)
Brennan	Eisenhower–1956	University of Pennsylvania	Harvard	Superior Court Judge, New Jersey (1); Appellate Division Judge (2)	
Whittaker	Eisenhower–1957		University of Kansas	U. S. Court of Appeals (1); U. S. District Judge (2)	
Stewart	Eisenhower–1958	Yale	Yale	U. S. Court of Appeals (4)	
Goldberg	Kennedy–1962	Northwestern	Northwestern	Counsel to AFL-CIO (13)	Secretary of Labor
White	Kennedy–1962	University of Colorado	Yale	Deputy Attorney General (1)	
Fortas	Johnson–1965	Southwestern College	Yale	Deputy Attorney General (2)	Undersecretary of Interior
Marshall	Johnson–1967	Lincoln University	Howard	U. S. Court of Appeals (4); Solicitor General (2)	NAACP Legal Defense Fund (21)
Burger	Nixon–1969	University of Minnesota	St. Paul College of Law	U. S. Court of Appeals (13); Assistant Attorney General (3)	Professor, Mitchel Law College (17)
Blackmun	Nixon–1970	Harvard	Harvard	U. S. Court of Appeals (11)	Professor, St. Paul College of Law (6)
Powell	Nixon–1971	Washington and Lee	Harvard		President, American Bar Association
Rehnquist	Nixon–1971	Stanford	Stanford	Assistant Attorney General	

[a]The basic information was obtained from Harold W. Chase and Craig R. Ducat, *Constitutional Interpretation* (St. Paul, Minn.: West Publishing Co., 1974), pp. 1361-76; and William B. Lockhart, et al., *Constitutional Law* (St. Paul, Minn.: West Publishing Co., 1970), pp. 1441-50.

[b]Denotes number of years serving in that capacity.

Table 3-2
Rankings of the Twenty-one Most Recent Justices[a]

Justice	Overall Ranking	Communication Skill Ranking						
		1.0	2.0	3.0	4.0	5.0	Median	Mean
Jackson	Near great	0	0	3	2	25	5.000	4.733
Harlan	Near great	0	1	0	5	24	5.000	4.733
Black	Great	0	0	3	11	17	5.000	4.733
Frankfurter	Great	1	0	0	11	13	4.273	4.129
Fortas	Near great	0	0	11	10	10	3.950	3.968
Warren	Great	0	3	8	11	9	3.909	3.839
Douglas	Near great	1	1	8	13	7	3.885	3.800
Brennan	Near great	0	2	9	13	7	3.846	3.806
Powell	Not rated	0	2	10	12	7	3.792	3.774
Stewart	Average	0	0	12	12	6	3.750	3.800
Rehnquist	Not rated	4	2	9	10	6	3.550	3.387
Marshall	Average	0	3	14	10	3	3.357	3.433
Burger	Not rated	2	3	13	11	2	3.308	3.258
White	Average	0	3	16	9	1	3.219	3.276
Goldberg	Average	1	4	16	7	2	3.125	3.167
Clark	Average	0	4	18	6	2	3.111	3.200
Minton	Failure	1	12	16	0	0	3.000	2.517
Blackmun	Not rated	5	5	11	7	2	2.955	2.867
Reed	Average	2	5	17	4	1	2.941	2.897
Burton	Failure	0	10	17	2	1	2.794	2.800
Whittaker	Failure	10	8	10	1	0	2.063	2.069

[a]The Spearman rank-order correlation matrix is as follows:

	Median	Mean
Overall	.89	.88
Median	–	.98

All correlations are significant at $p < .001$.

deans and professors of law, history, and political science were asked to evaluate the performance of the ninety-six justices who served on the Court from 1789-1969. Three of the justices during the period under consideration were ranked as great: Black, Frankfurter, and Warren. Five were ranked as near great: Douglas, Jackson, Harlan, Brennan, and Fortas. Six were ranked as average: Reed, Clark, Stewart, White, Goldberg, and Marshall. None were ranked as below average, but three—Burton, Minton, and Whittaker—were ranked as failures. Of the six rated as average, some may be underrated. This is most likely to be true of Justice Clark.[16] Furthermore, Justice Reed, although not colorful, was a hard-working and dedicated member of the Court, writing over three hundred opinions during his tenure of office. Justice Stewart has performed well as evidenced by the fact that President Nixon seriously considered him for promotion to the chief justice-ship. He had impeccable credentials when appointed, as did Justices White, Goldberg, and Marshall. Justice Stewart had graduated from Yale University cum laude and was a member of Phi Beta Kappa. Justice White may also be under-rated.[17] It is noteworthy that before his appointment, the former Rhodes Scholar and Phi Beta Kappa member was a deputy attorney general of the United States.

There appears to be some degree of consensus among scholars that had Justice Goldberg remained on the Court for a longer period of time, eventually he would have been ranked much higher. As for Justice Marshall, if the rankings had been based on civil liberties areas alone, it is clear that his position would have been elevated considerably. Furthermore, as one observer of the Court has noted, "Probably no other Justice ever came to the Supreme Court with so much experience in constitutional law as Thurgood Marshall."[18]

The three justices most clearly lacking in overall performance were Justices Burton, Minton, and Whittaker. The first two are acknowledged "cronies" of their appointer, President Truman. Justice Burton's ratings have been challenged by some students of the Court,[19] but in no respect could the three be rated above the category "below average." Oddly enough, all three had excellent credentials. Minton had practiced law for eighteen years and had served as a judge on the Seventh Circuit Court of Appeals for eight years. He had also served a term as U. S. senator from Indiana. Similarly, Justice Burton had been U. S. senator. He was also a mayor of Cleveland and had practiced law for twenty-three years. He was a Phi Beta Kappa graduate of Bowdoin College and Harvard University. Justice Whittaker had practiced law for thirty-one years and had been a United States district judge for two years before being elevated to the Court of Appeals for the Eighth Judicial Circuit. Eight months later, he was appointed by President Eisenhower to the Supreme Court. As one notable scholar has written, "on the basis of background and experience, [Whittaker] gave every promise of becoming an outstanding Justice."[20] In sum, these three appointments simply illustrate the fact that past behavior is not always indicative of future performance. Perhaps in these cases is found an illustration of the "Peter Principle" at work in the judicial appointments process.[21] It is simply impossible to screen out every appointee who will not make an exceptionally competent justice.

The Writing Skills of Supreme Court Justices

Columns 3-9 of Table 3-2 report the findings of a second survey, one specifically undertaken for the present study. Sixty names were drawn from the list of constitutional law professors in the United States, published by the Association of American Law Schools.[22] The respondents were asked the following question:

How would you evaluate each of the following justices's ability to communicate his ideas in written opinions? (Note: There are probably several justices with whom one disagrees ideologically, but nevertheless rank high in writing skill. Additionally, it may be that all of the justices fit into one or two categories.)

Respondents were given the choice of rating each justice's communication skills as very good (5), good (4), average (3), poor (2) and very poor (1). The justices in the table are ranked by median score.

Justices Jackson and Harlan clearly received the highest ratings. The former received a very good rating from twenty-five of thirty respondents, and the latter, from twenty-four of thirty. This is not unexpected as Justice Jackson has variously been referred to as a "highly knowledgeable, technically proficient lawyer,"[23] whose opinions "reveal a fine literary style and verbal brilliance."[24] Of his communication skills, the late Rocco J. Tresolini concluded, "He wrote with clarity and freshness."[25] Justice Harlan has been equally praised by constitutional scholars. Blaustein and Mersky, for example, have noted that he was "greatly respected for his knowledge and craftsmanship."[26] Professor Tresolini has noted that his decisions were "well reasoned and extremely methodical."[27] Perhaps Professor Norman Dorsen has best summarized Harlan's skill:

Harlan will be remembered not only for his judicial philosophy, but for his impressive technical proficiency. He has blended wide learning, a clear and orderly style, and a capacity and willingness to work and rework his opinions. Few justices have so painstakingly or successfully explained their premises and line of argument, and few in the Court's entire history are as safe as he from the charge that judicial opinions are no more than fiats "accomplished by little or no effort to support them in reason."[28]

Justices Black and Frankfurter, evaluated overall as "great" in the Blaustein-Mersky study, each received very high ratings on communication skills. This again is not surprising, since both were among the most influential figures on the Court during their terms of tenure. Prominent scholars have noted that Black's opinions were characterized "by a simplicity of style and clarity,"[29] were "concise and vivid,"[30] and were "marked by distinctive habits of thought."[31] According to Eugene V. Rostow, "the freshness of Justice Black's views," and the "simple lucidity of style . . . made his writing an instrument of abiding power."[32] Likewise, Justice Frankfurter has been described as "a judicial craftsman, a master of prose style."[33]

The next seven justices, Fortas through Rehnquist, all received solid ratings on their communication skills. Perhaps somewhat surprising are the rankings of Justices Powell and Rehnquist, who have been on the Court for a relatively short period of time. Justice Fortas is generally regarded as brilliant, possessing "uncanny ability." Professor Abraham has concluded that his "scholarly and structured style, [and] his penchant for effective phrase-making" partially account for his overall ranking as a near great.[34] Biographer Fred Graham has concluded that his opinions are "thorough and scholarly."[35]

Although various scholars have expressed disappointment over the fact that some of Chief Justice Warren's opinions "were not delivered with more clarity and explicitness,"[36] it is acknowledged that he wrote at least five outstanding opinions: *Brown* v. *Board of Education*,[37] *Watkins* v. *United States*,[38] *Reynolds* v. *Sims*,[39] *Miranda* v. *Arizona*,[40] and *Powell* v. *McCormack*.[41] Nevertheless, it is generally conceded that his opinions lacked the "doctrinal threads" found in the decisions of Frankfurter and Black. *New York Times* columnist Anthony Lewis has concluded that this resulted in "a bland, square presentation of the particular problem. . . ."[42]

Justice Douglas, historically one of the most controversial members of the Court, is generally known for his fluid style in civil liberties cases, yet many believe that his "craftsmanship and technical competence do not match his courage or the correctness of his views."[43] Others view Douglas more favorably. Some have referred to his ideas as "eloquently articulated."[44] Most agree that he certainly had a "flair for style."[45]

Both Justices Brennan and Stewart were known for their writing skills before joining the Supreme Court. Justice Brennan's opinions were referred to as "clear [and] forceful" during his tenure on the New Jersey bench.[46] Justice Stewart gained a reputation for clear, concise, and "carefully crafted, lucid opinions," while serving on the Court of Appeals for the Sixth Circuit.[47]

Justices Marshall through Clark received ratings of slightly above average. Justices Marshall, Burger, and White received a substantial number of votes in the good and very good categories, although all three were generally perceived as having only average communication skills. The problem of accurately assessing Justices Burger and Goldberg is compounded by the fact that the former has served for only a short period of time, while the latter stepped down from the Court after only three years of service. Of Goldberg's opinions, it has been suggested that in the area of labor law, they "were consistently incisive and knowledgeable. . . ."[48] There is some argument about the quality of writing skills possessed by Justice Clark. One scholar has referred to him as "uninteresting and unintelligent,"[49] while another claims that his dissenting opinions were characterized by "clarity and vigor."[50] Perhaps a middle position is more reasonable, for he did in fact author major opinions in the fields of separation of powers and civil liberties.[51]

Justice Minton, the first of five justices receiving a below average mean score, did not receive any good or very good ratings. He did receive sixteen average ratings, but he also received twelve poor and one very poor ratings. It has been said of Justice Minton that he "did his share of work on the bench but wrote no opinions of lasting significance."[52] In all fairness, however, it must be remembered that he was in poor health and suffered from pernicious anemia throughout most of his seven-year tenure. Indeed, in the last year, before his early retirement, he was forced to use a cane and had difficulty concentrating on his work.[53]

Justice Reed similarly performed his share of work while on the Court. For example, biographer F. William O'Brien has noted that he wrote 25 percent of the forty most important cases during the 1952-1953 term.[54] Nevertheless, as with Justice Minton, it has been said of his opinions that the language was "singularly uninspired."[55]

Justice Blackmun, the first Justice not to attain a median score of average (3.0), fared poorly compared to the other Nixon appointees. However, as with Burger, Powell, and Rehnquist, it is probably too early to arrive at a responsible judgment.

Justice Burton, who ranked next-to-last, oddly enough did not receive any failure ratings, and he did receive two good and one very good ratings. Perhaps the latter are due to the fact that his opinions, as Professor Tresolini has noted, "were characterized by thoroughness and conscientious attention to technical details."[56] On the other hand, the general consensus appears to be that the label, "least-able-in-a-century," once attached to his name, is not totally unfitting.[57] Despite hard work he managed to produce only five or six majority opinions a year, and according to one biographer, there "was not a tricky phrase in the lot."[58]

Last in median and mean scores is Justice Whittaker. Ranked as a failure overall, he also received ten ratings as a failure in his ability to communicate. As a biographer of Whittaker has suggested, "He was neither a judicial thinker nor a legal technician. None of his opinions showed any new insights. They were pedestrian."[59] In his brief tenure on the Court, he managed to average little more than one opinion a year.

It is interesting to note that the correlation between the overall rankings and the communication skills rankings is very high. Generally those justices achieving a high overall ranking were also those who ranked high on communication skills. However, three near greats, Harlan, Jackson, and Fortas, did achieve higher evaluations in writing skills than did Chief Justice Warren, who ranked overall as great. On the other hand, Justice Reed, rated overall as average, fell below Justice Minton (an overall failure) in communication skills.

To summarize, only five justices fell below average on the mean score and only four on the median score. Two of the latter, Justices Whittaker and Blackmun, served or have served only short periods of time, making evaluation difficult. Thus, it generally appears that the encoders of Supreme Court decisions are perceived as being unusually competent in their ability to communicate ideas. Indeed, the somewhat glowing picture presented above suggests that justices are rather effective writers. After all, the survey of leading law school professors juxtaposed alongside the comments of biographers is highly supportive of the hypothesis.

A strong note of caution is in order, however. It would be extremely misleading to leave the reader with the impression that the message (opinions) themselves are always, or indeed even generally, written in a language and style that is beyond reproach. In the first place, as Professor Henry Hart has suggested, "neither at the bar nor among the faculties of the law schools is there an adequate tradition of sustained, disinterested, and competent criticism of the

the professional quality of the Court's opinions."[60] The survey results thus may in part be based on superficial impressions, rather than detailed examinations, of the messages. Moreover, there is a major distinction between asking law school professors to evaluate a "justice's *ability* to communicate ideas in written opinions," and asking them to evaluate the craftsmanship of those opinions. In other words, a justice may be perceived by academics as "getting his message across" and therefore be considered an effective encoder, even though from a literary standpoint, the opinion is surprisingly convoluted and imprecise.

Second, it should be noted that not all biographers are entirely disinterested, objective conduits of information. Indeed, at least some of the laudatory comments extracted from their works may reflect the inherent bias often found in such undertakings. Moreover, as we have observed, a number of the justices are acknowledged poor writers. These facts, coupled with a recognition that even the most skillful justices on occasion do not live up to the expectations placed on them, indicate that on close scrutiny, the particular messages *themselves* may be of considerably poorer quality than the foregoing analysis might suggest.

Conclusions

Of the three hypotheses suggested at the beginning of this chapter, the first two are strongly confirmed. It is clear that Supreme Court justices are highly respected in this country and come from backgrounds and have experience that indicate that they are very well educated, well-informed, and exceedingly competent individuals. Indeed, as Professor Abraham has written, "discounting rare individual exceptions . . . the calibre of those who have attained service on the Court has been universally high and often indeed superior. . . . No other segment of American Government can match its general record of competence, achievement, and hard personalized labor."[61]

The third hypothesis is more vexatious. The consensus among scholars appears to be that Supreme Court justices effectively communicate their decisions. On the other hand, there is some reason to suspect these assessments. What is fairly obvious is that most justices possess a keen ability to encode decisions. Whether they actually and regularly maximize this ability, however, is investigated in the next chapter.

Notes

1. Daniel Berman, *It Is So Ordered* (New York: W. W. Norton, 1966), p. 41.

2. John Frank, *Marble Palace: The Supreme Court in American Life* (New York: Alfred A. Knopf, 1968), pp. 117-18.

3. See especially, William Rehnquist, "Who Writes Decisions of the Supreme Court?," *U. S. News and World Report,* December 13, 1957, pp. 74-75.

4. Ernest Friesen, Edward Gallas, and Nesta Gallas, *Managing the Courts* (Indianapolis: Bobbs-Merrill, 1972), p. 14.

5. See, e.g., W. A. Anderson, "Occupational Attitudes and Choices of a Group of College Men," *Social Forces,* 6 (December 1927, March 1928), 278-83, 467-73; Emory Bogardus, "Occupational Distance," *Sociology and Social Research,* 13 (September-October 1928), 73-81; George S. Counts, "The Social Status of Occupations: A Problem in Vocational Guidance," *School Review,* 33 (January 1925), 16-27; Walter Couter, "The Relative Prestige of Twenty Professions as Judged by Three Groups of Professional Students," *Social Forces,* 14 (May 1936), 522-29; H. C. Lehman and Paul A. Witty, "Further Study of the Social Status of Occupations," *Journal of Educational Sociology,* 5 (October 1931), 101-12; and Forrest Wilkinson, "Social Distance Between Occupations," *Sociology and Social Research,* 13 (January-February 1929), 234-44.

6. Mapheus Smith, "An Empirical Scale of Prestige Status Occupations," *American Sociological Review,* 8 (April 1943), 185-92.

7. Cecil North and Paul Hatt, "Jobs and Occupations: A Popular Evaluation," *Opinion News,* 9 (September 1, 1947), 3-13. For an analysis of the NORC study see Albert J. Reiss, *Occupations and Social Status* (New York: Free Press of Glencoe, 1961).

8. Robert Hodge, et al., "Occupational Prestige in the United States, 1925-63," *American Journal of Sociology,* 70 (November 1964), 286-302.

9. See, e.g., C. Wright Mills, *Power, Politics and People* (New York: Oxford University Press, 1963), p. 199.

10. John Schmidhauser, *The Supreme Court: Its Politics, Personalities and Procedures* (New York: Holt, Rinehart and Winston, 1960), p. 31.

11. Ibid., p. 34.

12. Ibid., p. 43.

13. John Schmidhauser, "The Justices of the Supreme Court: A Collective Portrait," *Midwest Journal of Political Science,* 3 (February 1959), 23.

14. Henry J. Abraham, *Justices and Presidents* (New York: Oxford University Press, 1974), pp. 43-44.

15. The poll was first published in *Life Magazine*, October 15, 1971, pp. 52-59. An enlarged version appeared in the *American Bar Association Journal,* 58 (November 1972), 1183-87.

16. Abraham, *supra* note 14, p. 224.

17. Ibid., p. 257.

18. Thomas R. Dye, *The Politics of Equality* (New York: The Bobbs-Merrill Co., Inc., 1971), p. 170.

19. Abraham, *supra* note 14.

20. Ibid., p. 247.

21. Laurence J. Peter and Raymond Hull, *The Peter Principle* (New York: W. Morrow, 1969).

22. *Directory of American Law Schools* (St. Paul, Minn.: West Publishing Co., 1973), p. 737.

23. Albert P. Blaustein and Roy Mersky, "Rating Supreme Court Justices," *American Bar Association Journal,* 58 (November 1972), 1186.

24. Rocco J. Tresolini, *American Constitutional Law* (New York: Macmillan Co., 1965), p. 748.

25. Ibid. For similar comments see Eugene Gerhart, *America's Advocate: Robert H. Jackson* (Indianapolis: Bobbs-Merril Co., 1958), p. 300.

26. Blaustein and Mersky, *supra* note 23.

27. Tresolini, *supra* note 24, p. 746.

28. Norman Dorsen, "John Marshall Harlan," in Leon Friedman and Fred L. Israel (eds.), *The Justices of the United States 1789-1969* (New York: Chelsea House Publishers, 1969), Vol. 4, p. 2819. Similarly, Wasby has stated that Harlan was "perhaps the Court's most respected opinion-writer." Stephen Wasby, *Continuity and Change: From the Warren Court to the Burger Court* (Pacific Palisades, Cal.: Goodyear Publishing Co., 1976), p. 19.

29. Tresolini, *supra* note 24, p. 735. See also John Frank, *Mr. Justice Black, the Man and His Opinions* (New York: Alfred A. Knopf, 1949), p. 136.

30. *The Supreme Court, Justice and the Law* (Washington: Congressional Quarterly, 1973), p. 26.

31. Eugene V. Rostow, "Mr. Justice Black: Some Introductory Observations," *Yale Law Journal,* 65 (February 1956), 452.

32. Ibid. See also, Frank, *supra* note 2, p. 132.

33. Abraham, *supra* note 14, p. 210, quoting *New York Times,* February 24, 1965, p. 40. For a concise analysis of Frankfurter's writings see Helen Thomas, *Felix Frankfurter: Scholar on the Bench* (Baltimore: Johns Hopkins Press, 1960), Chapter 15.

34. Ibid., p. 264.

35. Fred Graham, "Abe Fortas," in Friedman and Israel, *supra* note 28, p. 3024.

36. Abraham, *supra* note 14, p. 240.

37. 347 U. S. 483 (1954).

38. 354 U. S. 178 (1957). But see Anthony Lewis, "The Supreme Court and the Critics," *Minnesota Law Review,* 45 (January 1961), 305, 321.

39. 377 U. S. 533 (1964).

40. 384 U. S. 436 (1966).

41. 395 U. S. 486 (1969).

42. Anthony Lewis, "Earl Warren," in Friedman and Israel, *supra* note 28, p. 2724.

43. Blaustein and Mersky, *supra* note 23, at 1186. See also Wasby, *supra* note 28, p. 21.

44. Abraham, *supra* note 14, p. 210.

45. John P. Frank, "William O. Douglas," in Friedman and Israel, *supra* note 28, p. 2468.

46. Francis McQuade and Alexander T. Kardos, "Mr. Justice Brennan and His Legal Philosophy," *Notre Dame Lawyer,* 33 (May 1958), 321-49.

47. See Abraham, *supra* note 14, p. 249; Tresolini, *supra* note 24, p. 754. See also Jerold H. Israel, "Potter Stewart," in Friedman and Israel, *supra* note 28, p. 2937.

48. Stephen J. Friedman, "Arthur J. Goldberg," in Friedman and Israel, *supra* note 28, p. 2990.

49. Fred Rodell, *Nine Men* (New York: Random House, 1955), p. 311.

50. Tresolini, *supra* note 24, p. 740.

51. Abraham, *supra* note 14, p. 229. See also, Richard Kirkendall, "Tom C. Clark," in Friedman and Israel, *supra* note 28, p. 2676.

52. Abraham, ibid., p. 232.

53. Richard Kirkendall, "Sherman Minton," in Friedman and Israel, *supra* note 28, pp. 2707-08.

54. F. William O'Brien, *Justice Reed and the First Amendment* (Washington, D. C.: Georgetown University Press, 1958), p. 4.

55. Wesley McCune, *The Nine Young Men* (New York: Harper and Brothers, 1947), p. 65.

56. Tresolini, *supra* note 24, p. 737.

57. Rodell, *supra* note 49, p. 310. But see Richard Kirkendall, "Harold Burton," in Friedman and Israel, *supra* note 28, p. 2468.

58. McCune, *supra* note 55, p. 230.

59. Quoted in Blaustein and Mersky, *supra* note 23, at 1187.

60. Henry Hart, Jr., "The Supreme Court 1958 Term, Foreword: The Time Chart of the Justices," *Harvard Law Review*, 73 (November 1959), 125.

61. Henry J. Abraham, "Attaining Membership on the Court: Facts and Fantasies in the Appointment Process," (Paper presented to the Southern Political Science Association, 1974), p. 3.

4

The Messages: Supreme Court Opinions

Before launching into a discussion about the quality of Supreme Court messages, it will be helpful to briefly review the substantive content of the decisions referred to throughout this book.

The Substance of Recent Supreme Court Opinions

The Supreme Court opinions referred to in subsequent chapters may be placed in four general categories: defendants' rights, school integration, religion, and miscellaneous.

Defendants' Rights

One of the most controversial arenas of activity during the Warren Court was that involving the rights of defendants. In 1952 the Vinson Court had ruled that it is unconstitutional to pump a person's stomach to obtain incriminating evidence. A suspect and his wife had been sitting on the edge of a bed when police entered the room they were occupying. The man immediately swallowed two pills that were thought to be narcotics. The police handcuffed him, took him to the hospital, and ordered a physician to retrieve the capsules. In *Rochin* v. *California*,[1] Justice Frankfurter, writing for the Court, held that this conduct "shocked the conscience." The method was "too close to the rack and the screw to permit of constitutional differentiation."[2]

    The idea that one's body cannot be invaded to obtain evidence, however, was broadly reinterpreted by the Warren Court five years later. In *Breithaupt* v. *Abram*,[3] the Court held that a blood sample taken from an unconscious person who had been involved in a fatal automobile accident was constitutionally admissible as evidence in a court of law. Justice Clark noted that the procedure was performed "under the protective eye of a physician" and that blood tests had become a routine and unquestioned occurrence in American society. Thus, the procedure was not repugnant as in *Rochin*.

    The first widely disputed decision in the defendants' rights area was rendered in 1961. In *Mapp* v. *Ohio*,[4] the Court held the federal exclusionary rule applicable to the states. In essence the rule holds that illegally obtained evidence is inadmissible in court of law.[5] Thus, evidence obtained by the police in Ms. Mapp's home without a search warrant was ordered suppressed. Six years later the Court issued another momentous decision and again expounded upon "The right of the people to be secure in their persons, houses, papers, and effects, *against unreasonable searches and seizures, . . .*"[6] In *Katz* v. *United States,*[7] it was held that the fourth amendment "protects people, not places."[8] Thus, without a warrant, the evidence obtained from a listening device placed on the exterior of a telephone booth to monitor the conversations of an alleged gambler was held inadmissible.

In other cases, the Court held that certain searches without warrants are nontheless permissible. In one of its most important decisions aiding law enforcement officers in the performance of their duties, *Terry* v. *Ohio,*[9] the Court upheld the right of police to "stop and frisk" suspects:

. . . where a police officer observes unusual conduct which leads him reasonably to conclude in light of his experience that criminal activity may be afoot and that the persons with whom he is dealing may be armed and presently dangerous; where in the course of investigating this behavior he identifies himself as a policeman and makes reasonable inquiries; and where nothing in the initial stages of the encounter serves to dispell his reasonable fear for his own or others' safety, he is entitled for the protection of himself and others in the area to conduct a carefully limited search of the outer clothing of such persons in an attempt to discover weapons which might be used to assault him. Such a search is reasonable . . . and any weapons seized may properly be introduced in evidence against the person from whom they were taken.[10]

Similarly, in two cases in 1973, *United States* v. *Robinson,*[11] and *Gustafson* v. *Florida,*[12] the Court upheld the searches of defendants that were incidental to a legal arrest. Both were eventually convicted of possessing drugs after they had been searched. The decisions were based on the idea that police officers have a right to protect themselves from potential harm.

The right of an indigent defendant to be provided with an attorney at state expense gained support during the 1950s and was finally granted constitutional status in the famous case of *Gideon* v. *Wainwright.*[13] Clarence Earl Gideon had been convicted of a felony; during his trial he had constantly asked for an attorney to represent him. The judge refused because under Florida law an indigent had the right to be provided with counsel only in capital cases. The U. S. Supreme Court, however, overruled an earlier decision[14] and held that the sixth amendment guaranteed the right in all felony cases. Nine years later, in *Argersinger* v. *Hamlin,*[15] the Court extended the right holding "that absent a knowing and intelligent waiver, no person may be imprisoned for any offense, whether classified as petty, misdemeanor, or felony, unless he was represented by counsel at his trial."[16]

During the interim between *Gideon* and *Argersinger,* one of the Court's most controversial and sweeping decisions was issued. In *Miranda* v. *Arizona,*[17] Chief Justice Warren, writing for a five-man majority, declared that:

Prior to any questioning, the person must be warned that he has a right to remain silent, that any statement he does make may be used as evidence against him, and that he has a right to the presence of an attorney, either retained or appointed.[18]

The following year the Court held that a lineup was a "critical stage" in the criminal process and as such, a defendant was entitled to counsel during the process. The suspect in this case had been indicted for a bank robbery and was subsequently identified in a lineup. No notice was given to his lawyer about the proceeding. At the trial the witnesses again identified Wade. On appeal, the Supreme Court in *United States* v. *Wade*,[19] held that there was a substantial risk that the absence of defense counsel at the lineup might jeopardize a defendant's right to a fair trial.

Several years after *Miranda* the Court moved to reduce its impact. In *Harris* v. *New York*,[20] it held that although a confession made by a defendant before being issued the *Miranda* warnings could not be admitted as evidence at trial, it could be used to impeach his credibility as a witness if he took the stand.

Two defendants' rights cases, one during 1968 and the other in 1970, focused on the trial itself. In *Duncan* v. *Louisiana*,[21] the Court held that in all nonpetty cases, a defendant has the right to a trial by jury. In that case an offense punishable by two years' imprisonment, although the actual sentence levied was only 60 days and a $300 fine, was deemed to be serious. Two years later, in *Williams* v. *Florida*,[22] the Court held that Florida's practice of trying defendants accused of noncapital crimes before six-person juries was constitutional.

In 1972 the Court issued its long-awaited death penalty decision. In *Furman* v. *Georgia*,[23] the Court declared that, *as applied*, the penalty constituted cruel and unusual punishment in violation of the eighth and fourteenth amendments. It failed to declare the punishment cruel and unusual *per se*, but the immediate impact of the decision was to spare the lives of 631 men and women on death row.[24]

Finally, among the defendants' rights cases to be discussed in the forthcoming chapters are *In re Gault*,[25] and *Papachristou* v. *Jacksonville*.[26] In the former case the Court held that juveniles are entitled to adequate notice, the right to counsel, the right to confront their accusers, and a warning that they need not incriminate themselves. In essence juveniles were accorded "adult" status in these four areas. In the second case, the Court held that a loosely constructed vagrancy ordinance in Jacksonville, Florida was violative of the sixth amendment right to notice. It was deemed unconstitutional on account of its vagueness and overbreadth.

School Integration

Within months of assuming office, Chief Justice Warren wrote what can only be

labeled as one of the most controversial, yet indeed momentous, decisions issued
by the Court since the ill-fated *Dred Scott* opinion.[27] In *Brown* v. *Board of
Education I,*[28] the Court overruled its longstanding precedent in *Plessy* v.
Ferguson[29] and declared that "Separate educational facilities [for the races] are
inherently unequal."[30] Thus, school districts throughout the nation were put
on notice that their schools must be integrated. Although the decision was not
widely expected, a trend had clearly been established in that direction. In
Missouri ex rel. Gaines v. *Canada,*[31] the Court had declared that separate but
equal educational facilities must be provided within each state. Thus, the
practice of paying a black law student's expenses to travel and be educated in
another state was declared unconstitutional. Later, in *McLaurin* v. *Oklahoma,*[32]
the Court declared that once a student is admitted to school, in this case the
graduate school of education at the University of Oklahoma, he must be treated
on an equal basis. The practice of requiring McLaurin to sit at separate desks
adjoining the classrooms and separate tables outside the library reading room,
and eat at separate times in the school cafeteria, was held violative of the equal
protection clause of the fourteenth amendment.

That same year the Court deemphasized the word *separate* in the phrase
"separate but equal" and found that a law school established to provide blacks
with a legal education in Texas violated the Constitution because it could not
find "substantial equality in the educational opportunities offered white and
Negro law students by the State."[33] The ultimate result was to require the admission of blacks to the University of Texas law school.

Thus the opinion in *Brown I* had a modicum of precedent in former decisions.
The question remaining, however, was how to implement educational integration.
The following year in *Brown* v. *Board of Education II,*[34] the Court offered an
answer. The cases were to be remanded to the district courts for further hearings;
the courts were directed to enter such orders and decrees as were "necessary
and proper" to effect admission of students "to public schools on a racially
nondiscriminatory basis with *all deliberate speed....*"[35] By 1969 the Court was
intensely aggravated at the retarded pace with which integration was taking place.
Those opposing the decision had devised several ingenious schemes that delayed,
and in many instances terminated, the process of desegregation. However, in
Alexander v. *Holmes County Board of Education,*[36] Chief Justice Burger,
writing his first major opinion, ordered a denial of "all motions for additional
time." The standard "all deliberate speed" was replaced with a much more
exacting mandate: "The obligation of every school district is to terminate dual
school systems *at once* and to operate now and hereafter only unitary schools."[37]

Religion

In 1962 the Court, in *Engle* v. *Vitale,*[38] held that the recitation of a prayer written by the New York Board of Regents was unconstitutional. The devotion stated, "Almighty God, we acknowledge our dependence upon thee, and we beg Thy blessings upon us, our parents, our teachers and our Country." The Court held that the prayer violated the establishment clause of the first amendment. Despite the fact that the opinion aroused a storm of protest, it was but a mere indication of what was to come. The following year the Court issued an opinion in two cases, *Abington School District* v. *Schempp* and *Murray* v. *Curlett.*[39] It prohibited Bible reading and the recitation of the Lord's Prayer during morning exercises. As with the Board of Regents' prayer, these practices, too, were deemed violative of the first amendment establishment clause.

In 1971 the Court reviewed two additional cases in which the establishment of religion was a central point of concern. In *Lemon* v. *Kurtzman,*[40] it voided payment plans that provided parochial school teachers with salaries if they taught secular courses. That same day in *Tilton* v. *Richardson,*[41] the Court upheld the validity of federal grants to religiously affiliated colleges, provided they were not utilized for sectarian instruction, a place of worship, or "any part of the program of a school or department of divinity." The grants provided under the Higher Education Facilities Act were viewed as an aid to education and not religion, and as such did not violate the establishment clause of the first amendment.

Miscellaneous

During the 1960s the Court had occasion to review several reapportionment cases. Earlier it had refused to rule on the subject with several justices claiming that it involved political questions.[42] However, in 1962 the Court in *Baker* v. *Carr*[43] held that the radically malapportioned lower house of the Tennessee legislature denied the state's citizens equal protection of the law as guaranteed in the fourteenth amendment to the U. S. Constitution. In effect the Court mandated that the Tennessee House of Representatives be reapportioned. Two years later in *Reynolds* v. *Sims,*[44] the Court extended its ruling by applying the requirement to the upper house (Senate) of the Alabama legislature.

In 1970, in *Oregon* v. *Mitchell,*[45] the Court held that Congress had the authority to reduce the voting age for federal (but not state) elections and that it could abolish durational residency requirements for persons voting in presidential and vice-presidential elections. Two years later in *Dunn* v. *Blumstein,*[46] it held that there was no compelling interest on the part of Tennessee to require residency in the state for a year and in the county for three months before a citizen could vote. The statute was held unconstitutional. Thus in these two cases the Court carefully circumscribed state requirements that prevented a substantial number of the electorate from voting. In both instances the state was perceived as violating the equal protection clause of the fourteenth amendment.

In 1973 the court held, in *San Antonio* v. *Rodriguez*,[47] that states utilizing property tax schemes that ultimately allow one district to spend significantly larger amounts per pupil than others are constitutionally permissible, despite claims that the practice violates equal protection of the law.

During the same term of court the justices had an opportunity to rule on two abortion cases. In *Roe* v. *Wade*,[48] it declared unconstitutional a "Victorian" Texas law that forbade abortions except to save the life of the mother. In a companion case, *Doe* v. *Bolton*,[49] the more modern Georgia statute, which allowed the performance of an abortion after a large number of procedural requirements were satisfied, was declared violative of the constitution. Both opinions were justified on the pregnant woman's right of privacy as delineated in earlier decisions.

The final two cases, which are referred to in subsequent chapters of this text, were also issued in 1973. In *Miller* v. *California*,[50] and *Paris Adult Theater I* v. *Slaton*,[51] the Court reversed in part earlier obscenity rulings. They affirmed the *Roth*[52] holding that obscene material is not protected by the first amendment but held that such material need not be proven "*utterly* without redeeming social value," and that "contemporary community standards" need not be national standards. Thus, states were given greater authority to prevent the dissemination of materials determined to be obscene at the state level.

The Language and Style of the Opinion

Having reviewed the substantive content of the Supreme Court decisions referred to throughout this book, we now proceed to an examination of the quality of these messages.

Numerous scholars have noted that certain factors intrinsic to the opinion itself affect the communications process.[53] Theory would suggest that if the target public is to readily understand the message, it must be (1) written in an appropriate language and style, and (2) be issued at an appropriate time carrying an appropriate mandate.

Quality of Prose

Perhaps the foremost critic of the prose utilized by Supreme Court justices is John P. Frank. Indeed, when referring to the volumes of the U. S. Reports he has noted that "This mighty pile is, from the literary standpoint, explored approximately as much as Mount Everest."[54] He claims that critics are right and that "What appears to be a great literary wasteland is just that."[55] Frank concedes that there are some exceptions but deduces that opinions best fit into a category labeled "legal lumpy." As such they utilize "awkward English," are long, involved, clumsy, and wordy. Few would disagree with his characterization.

Indeed as D. W. Stevenson has suggested, "Over the years a number of law review articles — some very good ones — have asserted that opinions are too long, that they are filled with unnecessary detail, that they are overloaded with footnotes, that they are couched in jargon unclear to many of their readers, that they are poorly arranged and carelessly worded."[56]

Opinion Clarity

Richard Johnson has noted that "A concern with message *clarity* by the Court improves the chances for adequate transmission." He also observes that "If the message . . . is ambiguous, district and state judges will find many convenient openings, allowing them to hand down decisions which will not fly in the face of local values."[57] It might be added that not only will judges find loopholes, but law enforcement officers, county commissioners, and the whole range of target publics will do so as well. Harrell Rodgers and Charles Bullock agree. In their study of civil rights laws and their consequences, they note that "Vague laws have frequently allowed officials to claim that they were obedient when in fact they had changed their behavior very little."[58]

Examples of exceedingly clear opinions are abundant. Perhaps the most obvious is *Miranda* v. *United States.*[59] There, Chief Justice Earl Warren specifically enumerated what was expected of the police officer prior to the questioning of a defendant:

He must be warned prior to any questioning that he has the right to remain silent, that anything he says can be used against him in a court of law, that he has the right to the presence of an attorney, and that if he cannot afford an attorney one will be appointed for him prior to any questioning if he so desires.[60]

With such specificity there is little room for avoidance, evasion, or delay. The message is so clear that an offender is unlikely to escape penalty or punishment. As a result, there has been a high degree of technical compliance with the mandate of this decision.[61]

On the other hand, it is readily admitted that many of the Court's opinions are exceedingly ambiguous. For example, in *Dennis* v. *United States,*[62] the Court utilized "clear and present danger" language to uphold certain sections of the Smith Act. However, it is generally agreed that the rationale actually applied was Justice Sanford's "bad tendency" test.[63] Thus, there has been a great deal of confusion about the exact reasoning of the opinion.

An example of an extremely vague standard is found in the case of *Brown* v. *Board of Education II.*[64] Indeed, Rodgers and Bullock claim that one of the factors impeding integration during the first decade subsequent to the decision was the Court's failure to formulate specific standards to guide enforcement. This they viewed as "a serious mistake."[65] Indeed, the decision was filled with ambiguity. Such phrases as "all deliberate speed," "good faith," and "at the earliest possible date" are imprecise. However, it might be argued that ambiguity in this instance was entirely necessary. After all, the Court was certainly aware of the intense resentment to *Brown I* issued the year before.[66] There was every reason to believe that a clear-cut directive might lead to outright defiance if not rioting or civil war. The Court has generally recognized its dependence on other branches and levels of government for support. Without such backing, the "nine old men" can accomplish very little. Perhaps they feared that Jackson's legendary maxim would be applied to them. It will be recalled that upon hearing of the Court's decision in the Cherokee Nation Case[67] the president allegedly stated, "John Marshall has made his decision, now let him enforce it." Thus it appears that given certain circumstances the Court must necessarily be ambiguous. In dealing with integration a forthright decision might have accomplished far less than the opinion issued.

Opinion Conciseness

In recent years the number of written majority opinions has gradually risen. Accompanying this rise has been a rather dramatic increase in the number of written concurrences and dissents.[68] As a result, one might reasonably argue and even predict that the length of majority opinions should decline. However, this is clearly not the case. Table 4-1 illustrates a nearly continuous rise in the average number of pages per majority opinion. Thus, justices are not only writing more opinions these days, but they are writing longer ones as well. Some argue that this is because the Court is tackling more difficult, if not more important problems. Even if one assumes this explanation to be correct, and this author does not,[69] one need only look at Justice Blackmun's exceedingly redundant opinions in the abortion cases[70] to realize that the tendency to be verbose is ever present. As one scholar has pointed out, justices "inevitably fall at times into the snare of saying more than they need to say in an opinion."[71] Indeed, it is widely recognized that many opinions are permeated with a large quantity of dicta (judicial asides).

   Unanimous decisions are thought to convey the message more forcefully than split decisions. For example, it has been suggested that Chief Justice Earl Warren believed this to be exceedingly important and thus labored extensively to obtain a unanimous opinion in *Brown I*.[72] Historically this has been most easily accomplished when a large majority of the Court has consisted of justices with highly similar ideological orientations, such as during the early part of the twentieth century. On the other hand, when the Court has been ideologically split, such as during the later Warren and early Burger years, this is much more difficult to achieve.

   Split decisions, it is generally argued, weaken the thrust of the message.

Table 4-1
Length of Majority Opinionsa

Term	Number of Opinions	Total Number of Pages	Pages per Case
1949	87	793	9
1954	78	621	8
1959	96	1021	11
1964	91	1056	12
1969	83	1076	13
1974	122	2006	16

aThe length of each majority opinion was counted and rounded off to the nearest whole page. Excluded were concurring and dissenting opinions.

The concurring and dissenting opinions give dissidents a base from which to launch a case for noncompliance, evasion, or delay. Moreover, it is widely recognized that radically split decisions (5 to 4) may be easily overturned at a later date and thus should not be relied on to any great extent.

Dissents and concurrences often generate confusion about the main rationale of the decision. The *Furman* opinions certainly fit this description.[73] The per curiam opinion itself is a mere paragraph in length. However, there are five separate concurrences and four separate dissents, totaling 232 pages in all. Much was written about the decision immediately after its promulgation, and it is clear that there were many misperceptions about the rationale on which it is based.[74] It has been clarified by the Court to some extent in recent cases.[75] Nonetheless, there still remains a number of unanswered questions about its rationale.

Quality of Rationale

Recent criticism has been directed toward the Court for caring "too much about results and not enough about reasons."[76] For example, the late Alexander M. Bickel and his coauthor Harry Wellington have stated: "The Court's product has shown an increasing incidence of the sweeping dogmatic statement, of the formulation of results accompanied by little or no effort to support them in reason ... [and that they] frankly fail to build the bridge between the authorities they cite and the results they reach."[77] Similarly, Professor Henry Hart of the Harvard Law School has observed that "few of the Court's opinions, far too few, genuinely illuminate the area of the law with which they deal."[78]

No doubt, there is a great deal of truth in the above statements. In all

fairness, though, it must be pointed out that such attacks have been directed mainly at the activist Warren Court by adherents of judicial self-restraint. Thus,
underlying political motivations may be the catalyst for such criticism rather than
a genuine belief that justices generally "duck issues" and make "technical mis-
takes." Indeed, the only justice who has been consistently chastised for regularly
failing to ground his decisions in precedent is former Justice William O. Douglas.[79]
Furthermore, many justices also take cognizance of social science data that
support their opinion. For example, the reliance on social science data in
Brown v. *Board of Education*[80] was a major source of authority for the ruling.
Perhaps the importance of the famous footnote eleven has been over stated.[81]
However, one need only look at the *Furman* opinions to realize how extensive the
use of such literature has become.[82]

In further defense of the encoders it is suggested that their critics "often do
not take cognizance of the difficulties . . . under which Supreme Court Justices
labor."[83] There are pressures of time, which simply do not allow for a master-
fully written law review article on the subject. Moreover, the final opinion is often
the product of a number of compromises between several justices.[84] Naturally,
such a situation may produce rationale with "the vacuity characteristic of des-
perately negotiated documents."[85]

Attention to Encoders and Target Publics

It is generally conceded that Supreme Court opinions are not written for consump-
tion by the public-at-large.[86] Opinions often contain technical phrases unknown
to the average person. For example, Justice Frankfurter's opinions have been
referred to as "repositories for some of the most exotic words in the English
language."[87] As one biographer has stated, "Put briefly, Justice Frankfurter did
not write to be understood by newspaper readers."[88] His opinions simply were
"not meant for those untrained in the law or its sister disciplines."[89] Although
Frankfurter's style was uncharacteristically eloquent, it is not unique in terms of
those to whom it was directed. Indeed, this lack of concern for the general
audience is perhaps the greatest weakness in Supreme Court messages. It places
the responsibility of interpreting decisions squarely on the press, attorneys, and
other encoders. As Wasby has observed, when this situation occurs, "the
chances for misinterpretation (both purposeful and innocent) increase radically."[90]

The Timing and Mandate of the Opinion

Timing

The timing of Supreme Court decisions is particularly important in the communications process. Some decisions such as *Baker* v. *Carr*[91] and *Gideon* v. *Wainwright*[92] have apparently been long overdue. Others such as *Reynolds* v. *Sims*[93] and the school prayer cases[94] perhaps should have been delayed if the Court indeed follows the public opinion polls.[95] However, in the twentieth century the Court has been overruled by amendment only once.[96] Thus, it would appear that the Court's timing rarely has been radically inappropriate.

Perhaps more important than the timing itself is the number of opinions issued on any one day. If too many are delivered at once, reporters simply do not have the time to read and report them accurately. Thus, opinions are often misinterpreted and overgeneralized. Moreover, certain very important opinions may be completely overlooked. For example, the day *Engle* v. *Vitale*[97] was delivered, the Court issued sixteen other full opinions. Despite the importance of some of these, most were overlooked by reporters.[98]

Traditionally, Monday has been "Decision Day." It was, and is, this practice that places a tremendous strain on the communications process. In April 1965, Chief Justice Earl Warren indicated that the Court would begin issuing opinions throughout the week. However, as Wasby has reported, after initially following the change, the Court has continued to render most of its decisions on Monday.[99]

Mandate

Theory would indicate that the message may be more effective if it is self-executing, if it requires change of a negative kind, and if it reinforces a long series of decisions.[100] The Court has generally been very cautious not to require positive action on the part of federal, state, or local governments. No doubt this is in part due to President Jackson's maxim stated earlier. On the other hand, the Court has become deeply involved with prohibiting certain actions by these entities. It has demanded that states *stop* allowing prayers in the school, unequal application of the death penalty, segregation in the schools, discrimination in public accommodations, infringements on the right to vote, unreasonable searches and seizures, infringements on privacy and travel, and kangaroo court procedures.

The Court has also been very careful not to make radical departures from recent precedent.[101] For example, after the Court's decision in *Plessy* v. *Ferguson*,[102] there were literally dozens of intervening decisions before *Brown* was issued.[103] And it took another fifteen years before the Court abandoned the "all deliberate speed" requirement and replaced it with the "at once" standard.[104] Likewise, a long series of cases served as precedent for some of the most controversial decisions of the Warren Court: *Miranda, Katz, Schempp,* and *Curlett.*[105] Moreover, although the *Reynolds*[106] reapportionment decision had somewhat fewer precedents, *Baker* v. *Carr*[107] and *Gomillion* v. *Lightfoot*[108] did serve as precedent in many respects. Certainly the dozens of reapportionment cases since *Reynolds* have come as a surprise to very few.

Conclusions

It may be concluded that Supreme Court opinions leave much to be desired. Although they may be appropriately timed, carry an appropriate mandate and be grounded in precedent, they are often unclear, imprecise and written in unsatisfactory prose. Clearly, the most severe deficiency in the Court's messages is that they are not written in a manner which the public and many encoders can readily understand and interpret. This is particularly true in the cases involving civil liberties, an area that has an immediate and direct affect on the public. There simply is little reason for this to occur in an industrialized nation with a highly educated electorate. It is true that many in the legal profession claim that writing opinions in this manner is impossible. Nevertheless, there are a number of trial courts throughout the nation that have curbed the use of latin phraseology and restricted the use of technical rhetoric. In these situations there apparently have been few adverse effects. Likewise, at the appellate level justices could write for the educated public and forfeit very little, if anything, in terms of content. It may be that attorneys and jurists oppose the reform because of vested interests. After all, their livelihood and economic position depend to a great extent on restricting the number of individuals capable of dealing with legal issues. Moreover, their training dictates that they write in such a style.

On the other hand, more objective individuals may argue that the use of such technical language adds symbolically to the Court's prestige and thus enhances respect for the institution. The persuasiveness of such an argument, however, is seriously weakened in a modern, democratic state with a highly educated populace. It is very probable that in such situations courts gain greater respect if encoders and target publics understand how and why the justices arrive at their decisions.

Notes

1. 342 U. S. 165 (1952).
2. Ibid., at 172.
3. 352 U. S. 432 (1957).
4. 367 U. S. 643 (1961).
5. Weeks v. United States, 232 U. S. 383 (1914).
6. U. S. Constitution, Amend. 4.
7. 389 U. S. 347 (1967).
8. Ibid., at 351.
9. 392 U. S. 1 (1968).
10. Ibid., at 30-31.
11. 414 U. S. 218 (1973).
12. 414 U. S. 260 (1973).

13. 372 U. S. 335 (1963).

14. Betts v. Brady, 316 U. S. 455 (1942).

15. 407 U. S. 25 (1972).

16. Ibid., at 37.

17. 384 U. S. 436 (1966).

18. Ibid., at 472.

19. 388 U. S. 218 (1967).

20. 401 U. S. 222 (1971).

21. 391 U. S. 145 (1968).

22. 399 U. S. 78 (1970).

23. 408 U. S. 238 (1972).

24. For an extended analysis see Larry Berkson, *"Furman* v. *Georgia:* Initial Reaction and Immediate Impact," *Public Affairs Forum,* 5 (October 1975), 1-9.

25. 387 U. S. 1 (1967).

26. 405 U. S. 156 (1972).

27. Scott v. Sanford, 19 How. 393, 15 L.Ed. 691 (1857).

28. 347 U. S. 483 (1954).

29. 163 U. S. 537 (1896).

30. 347 U. S. 483, 495 (1954).

31. 305 U. S. 337 (1938).

32. 339 U. S. 637 (1950).

33. Sweatt v. Painter, 339 U. S. 629, 633 (1950).

34. 349 U. S. 294 (1955).

35. Ibid., at 301 (emphasis added).

36. 396 U. S. 19 (1969).

37. Ibid., at 20 (emphasis added).

38. 370 U. S. 421 (1962).

39. 374 U. S. 203 (1963).

40. 403 U. S. 602 (1971).

41. 403 U. S. 672 (1971).

42. Colegrove v. Green, 328 U. S. 549 (1946).

43. 369 U. S. 186 (1962).

44. 377 U. S. 533 (1964).

45. 400 U. S. 112 (1970).

46. 405 U. S. 330 (1972).

47. 411 U. S. 1 (1973).

48. 410 U. S. 197 (1973).

49. 410 U. S. 113 (1973).

50. 413 U. S. 15 (1973).

51. 413 U. S. 49 (1973).

52. Roth v. United States, 354 U. S. 476 (1957).

53. See, e.g., Stephen Wasby, "Getting the Message Across—Communicating

Court Decisions to the Police," *Justice System Journal,* 1 (Winter 1974), 29, 35-38.

54. John Frank, *Marble Palace: The Supreme Court in American Life* (New York: Alfred A. Knopf, 1968), p. 130.

55. Ibid.

56. D. W. Stevenson, "Writing Effective Opinions," *Judicature,* 59 (October 1975), 134.

57. Richard M. Johnson, *The Dynamics of Compliance: Supreme Court Decision-Making from a New Perspective* (Evanston, Ill.: Northwestern University Press, 1967), p. 26 (emphasis added).

58. Harrell Rodgers and Charles Bullock, *Law Social Change* (New York: McGraw-Hill Book Co., 1972), p. 199.

59. 384 U. S. 436 (1966).

60. Ibid., at 479.

61. See, e.g., Richard Medalie, et al., "Custodial Police Interrogation in Our Nation's Capitol: The Attempt to Implement Miranda," *Michigan Law Review,* 66 (May 1968), 1347-1422; and Michael Wald, et al., "Interrogations in New Haven: The Impact of Miranda," *Yale Law Journal,* 76 (July 1967), 1519-1648. Other decisions generally recognized as mandating precise action by the respondents were *Reynolds* v. *Sims,* 377 U. S. 533 (1964); *Duncan* v. *Louisiana,* 391 U. S. 145 (1968); *Gideon* v. *Wainwright,* 372 U. S. 335 (1963); *Roe* v. *Wade,* 410 U. S. 113 (1973); and *Doe* v. *Bolton,* 410 U. S. 179 (1973).

62. 341 U. S. 494 (1951).

63. The test originated in *Gitlow* v. *New York,* 268 U. S. 652 (1925). For an analysis see Henry J. Abraham, *Freedom and the Court* (New York: Oxford University Press, 1972), pp. 190-201.

64. 349 U. S. 294 (1955).

65. Rodgers and Bullock, *supra* note 58, p. 77.

66. Brown v. Board of Education, 347 U. S. 483 (1954).

67. Worcester v. Georgia, 6 Pet. 515 (1832).

68. See the November issues of the *Harvard Law Review* for a summary. See also, Gerhard Casper and Richard Posner, "A Study of the Supreme Court's Caseload," *The Journal of Legal Studies,* 3 (June 1974), 339-75; and Gregory Rathjen, "An Analysis of Separate Opinion Writing Behavior As Dissonance Reduction," *American Politics Quarterly,* 2 (October 1974), 393.

69. But see Anthony Lewis, "The Supreme Court and Its Critics," *Minnesota Law Review,* 45 (January 1961), 305, 325-29.

70. Roe v. Wade, 410 U. S. 113 (1973); and Doe v. Bolton, 410 U. S. 179 (1973).

71. Loren P. Beth, *Politics, The Constitution and the Supreme Court* (New York: Harper and Row, 1962), p. 46. See also Frank, *supra* note 54, p. 132; and Daniel Berman, *It Is So Ordered* (New York: W. W. Norton, 1966), pp. 114-15. For a thorough critique recommending shorter opinions, see Herbert Gregory, "Shorter Judicial Opinions," *Virginia Law Review,* 34 (1948), 362-70.

72. See, e.g., Berman, ibid., pp. 107-08. For further discussion of the following analysis see Stephen Wasby, *Continuity and Change: From the Warren Court to the Burger Court* (Pacific Palisades, Cal.: Goodyear Publishing Co., 1976), pp. 56-57.

73. Furman v. Georgia, 408 U. S. 238 (1972).

74. See Berkson, *supra* note 24.

75. Gregg v. Georgia, 428 U. S. 153, *reh. den.* 429 U. S. 875 (1976).

76. Lewis, *supra* note 69, at 320.

77. Alexander Bickel and Harry Wellington, "Legislative Purpose and the Judicial Process: The Lincoln Mills Case," *Harvard Law Review,* 71 (November 1957), 3.

78. Henry Hart, Jr., "The Supreme Court 1958 Term, Foreward: The Time Chart of the Justices," *Harvard Law Review,* 73 (November 1959), 100.

79. Eugene Gerhart, *America's Advocate: Robert H. Jackson* (Indianapolis: The Bobbs-Merrill Co., 1958), p. 297. For Justice Douglas' own comments on stare decisis see William O. Douglas, "Stare Decisis," *The Record of the Association of the Bar of the City of New York,* 4 (May 1949), 152-79.

80. 347 U. S. 483 (1954).

81. The text of the footnote is as follows:

K. B. Clark, Effect of Prejudice and Discrimination on Personality Development (Midcentury White House Conference on Children and Youth, 1950); Witmer and Kotinsky, Personality in the Making (1952), c. VI; Deutscher and Chein, The Psychological Effects of Enforced Segregation: A Survey of Social Science Opinion, 26 J. Psychol. 259 (1948); Chein, What are the Psychological Effects of Segregation Under Conditions of Equal Facilities?, 3 Int. J. Opinion and Attitude Res. 229 (1949); Brameld, Educational Costs, in Discrimination and National Welfare (Mac Iver, ed., 1949), 44-48; Frazier, The Negro in the United States (1949), 674-681. And see generally Myrdal, An American Dilemma (1944). 347 U. S. 483, 494-95 (1953).

82. Furman v. Georgia, 408 U. S. 238 (1972).

83. Lewis, *supra* note 69, at 324.

84. See Gerhart, *supra* note 79, p. 289.

85. Bickel and Wellington, *supra* note 77.

86. See also, Frank, *supra* note 54, p. 131.

87. Helen Thomas, *Felix Frankfurter: Scholar on the Bench* (Baltimore: Johns Hopkins Press, 1960), p. 343.

88. Ibid.

89. Ibid., p. 345.

90. Stephen Wasby, *The Impact of the United States Supreme Court* (Homewood, Ill.: The Dorsey Press, 1970), p. 84.

91. 369 U. S. 186 (1962).

92. 372 U. S. 335 (1963).

93. 377 U. S. 533 (1964).

94. Abington School District v. Schempp, 374 U. S. 203 (1963); and Murray v. Curlett, 374 U. S. 179 (1963).

95. See Walter Murphy, *Congress and the Court* (Chicago: University of Chicago Press, 1965), pp. 262-66. Justice White was very concerned in this respect. See Wasby *supra* note 72, p. 22.

96. U. S. Constitution, Amend. 16.

97. 370 U. S. 421 (1962).

98. Chester Newland, "Press Coverage of the United States Supreme Court," *Western Political Quarterly,* 17 (March 1964), 32. See also John MacKenzie, "The Warren Court and the Press," *Michigan Law Review,* 67 (December 1968), 305-06. There he points out that the decisions and orders of June 12, 1967, the final day of the term, are printed in Volume 388 of the U. S. *Reports* which exceeds 580 pages.

99. See Wasby, *supra* note 90, pp. 86-87.

100. See Joel Grossman, "The Supreme Court and Social Change," *American Behavioral Scientist,* 4 (March/April 1970), 545-46.

101. A notable exception is the second of the flag salute cases. See Minersville School District v. Gobitis, 310 U. S. 586 (1940); and West Virginia State Board of Education v. Barnette, 319 U. S. 624 (1943). But see, Robert M. Spector, "Judicial Biography and the U. S. Supreme Court: A Bibliographical Appraisal," *American Journal of Legal Education,* 2 (January 1967), 1.

102. 163 U. S. 537 (1896).

103. See, e.g., Sweatt v. Painter, 339 U. S. 629 (1950); McLaurin v. Oklahoma, 339 U. S. 637 (1950); Sipuel v. Oklahoma, 332 U. S. 631 (1948); and Missouri *ex rel.* Gaines v. Canada, 305 U. S. 676 (1938).

104. See Brown v. Board of Education II, 349 U. S. 294 (1955); and Alexander v. Holmes County Board of Education, 396 U. S. 19 (1969).

105. Miranda v. Arizona, 384 U. S. 436 (1966); Katz v. United States, 389 U. S. 347 (1968); Abington School District v. Schempp, 374 U. S. 203 (1963); and Murray v. Curlett, 374 U. S. 179 (1963).

106. Reynolds v. Sims, 377 U. S. 533 (1964).

107. 369 U. S. 186 (1962).

108. 364 U. S. 339 (1960).

5 The Channels of Communication

Numerous studies have been undertaken to determine perceptions about the utility, reliability, credibility, and desirability of the various media in communicating news. For example, the Roper Organization has repeatedly questioned interviewees in national survey samples about which of the media are preferred. In 1972 it was found that respondents favored television (64 percent) over newspapers (50 percent), radio (21 percent), and magazines (8 percent). Television was also widely perceived as being the most credible source of news information (48 percent), followed by newspapers (21 percent), magazines (10 percent), and radio (8 percent).[1]

Despite studies by Roper and others, very little is known about the channels by which Supreme Court decisions are transmitted to specific publics. To fill this void, each respondent in this survey was asked to identify the channels by which he usually obtained such information. Before analyzing the statistical findings, it is necessary to make a few introductory remarks about the various channels suggested.

Radio and Television

The broadcast media generally have had great difficulty in following the work of the Supreme Court. The primary obstacle has been the insistence of the Court that cameras and broadcasting equipment be prohibited in the courtroom. The justices have been supported in their position by Newton Minow, former Federal Communications commissioner. Along with coauthors Martin and Mitchell, he argues that television coverage of actual Supreme Court proceedings would inflame controversy, divide the country, "diminish the Court's prestige and throw the Court . . . into the whirlpool of controversial political television."[2]

Despite the debatable assumptions of this view, it is strictly adhered to in practice. Broadcast organizations have not been allowed to present live coverage of oral arguments or opinion reading, perhaps two of the most interesting aspects of courtroom procedure. As a result, until recently there has been only limited coverage of the Court by this media. However, a counter trend may be taking place. Although live coverage of the Court appears out of the question, there has been some movement toward television interviews with the justices themselves.[3] Further, during the "Watergate" crisis, Fred Graham was hired by CBS News to cover the Court's activities.[4]

Nonetheless, today there is still no radio or television network that assigns a full-time correspondent to the Court. Indeed, in a survey conducted by Everette Dennis in January 1974, no regular or even semiregular attendance by members of the broadcast media was found. Only Fred Graham of CBS, Carl Stern of NBC, and Dan Garcia of ABC "occasionally" attend the Court.[5]

Even if additional personnel were assigned to the Court and they appeared with greater regularity, the broadcast medium has inherent limitations that impede its effectiveness as a channel for communicating Supreme Court decisions. At most, a minute or two may be devoted to the story, forcing oversimplification and technical inaccuracies. Moreover, if "noise" enters the process, either mechanically in the media (static, power failure) or in the form of an environmental distraction to the receiver (children playing, doors slamming), the communication network breaks down.[6]

Newspapers

David L. Grey has suggested that "The role of the press is . . . primary in the early flow of information and resulting opinion on what the Court has said."[7] The suggestion has been substantiated by the investigations of Neal Milner. He found that police officers in four Wisconsin cities ranked newspapers no lower than third in a list of eleven "first sources of information" about the *Miranda* decision.[8] Similarly, in Florida nearly every one of the publics examined relied heavily on newspapers as sources of information about Supreme Court decisions. The most popular were state newspapers: *Gainesville Sun, Jacksonville Times Union, Miami Herald, Orlando Sentinel, St. Petersburg Times, Tallahassee Democrat,* and *Tampa Tribune.* However, mention was made of three national newspapers: *Christian Science Monitor, New York Times,* and *Wall Street Journal.*

There are several drawbacks to utilizing newspapers as a channel of information. Historically few personnel have been assigned to cover the work of the Court. As Max Freedman has written, the "Supreme Court is the worst reported . . . institution in the American system of government."[9] For example, Everette Dennis notes that only three members of the press and four wire service reporters regularly attend sessions of the Court.[10] Thus the public is not exposed to a wide variety of interpretations. As Chester Newland has suggested, this is extremely important because "the burden of sorting, digesting and reporting the information about the Supreme Court is left almost entirely to the newsman . . . ."[11] Furthermore, nearly all reporters have broader responsibilities and often must report the activities of other governmental units. Thus they cannot devote the requisite time to analyze Supreme Court decisions.

Second, experienced reporters are not assigned to the Supreme Court. In 1964, for example, Newland found that most were untrained in reporting legal

matters.[12] In 1974, the situation remained the same. Dennis reports that although
there was an average experience level of approximately 11.5 years, most of the
current reporters had "general-assignment" backgrounds.[13] Thus, novices were
being utilized to interpret complex opinions, which are difficult even for attorneys and law school professors to comprehend. Moreover, Dennis found their
tenures to be very brief, amounting to an average of little more than 2.5 years.
Thus, it appears that about the time reporters become proficient and skillful in
covering the Supreme Court, they move on to different assignments.

Third, the conditions under which reporters operate are not conducive to
high-quality reporting. They are under tremendous pressure to meet the dead-
lines of afternoon papers, and they must make rapid judgments about large quan-
tities of material without the benefit of prior briefings.[14] Moreover, the Court
has a strong tradition of not catering to the needs of the media. Indeed, unlike
congressmen and the president, the justices do not provide a vast array of public
relations materials to the press. Opinions are simply handed out from the
clerk's office without accompanying comments. As one close observer of the
Court has stated, "The Supreme Court is about as oblivious as it is conceivable
to be" in matters concerning public relations.[15] This observation has lead another observer to conclude that it is this "obliviousness" which accounts in large
measure for "the fact Supreme Court reporting is not all that it should or could
be."[16] Similarly John MacKenzie, Supreme Court reporter for the *Washington Post*
has described the relationship between the Court and press as "perhaps the most
primitive arrangement in the entire communications industry for access to an
important source of news material . . . ."[17] Naturally the situation leads to many
distortions, inaccuracies, and oversights. For example, Stephen Wasby has noted
that certain newspapers carried a report that the Supreme Court had outlawed segregation on intrastate buses, when it actually had not done so. Despite printed re-
tractions the next day, officials in eleven cities ordered an end to the segregation.[18]

Another unfortunate condition under which some reporters labor is the
pressure exerted by sales-conscious editors to select sensational material over the
more important cases.

A fourth problem is that relatively few newspapers carry extensive information about Supreme Court decisions. As Daniel Berman has written, "The same
media that are packed with news of presidential and congressional actions provide only the most meager coverage of developments in the Court."[19] For example, after analyzing press coverage of the Court's October 1961 term, Chester
Newland concluded that detailed and informative reporting is found in only three
newspapers: the *New York Times,* the *Washington Evening Star,* and the *Washington Post.*[20] A more recent study reaffirms this conclusion by noting that in
1974 only these three papers assigned reporters to regularly cover the work of
the Court.[21]

A fifth drawback is that wire services are relied on to a great extent by the
press for its information. For example, Newland found that most of the

sixty-three leading metropolitan daily newspapers relied on this source for information about the reapportionment and school prayer decisions. Thus, the mistake of a single wire service reporter may result in the delivery of incorrect information to a large segment of society. This problem is compounded by the fact that recent estimates suggest that over half of all American newspapers obtain *all* their information about the Supreme Court from a single wire service: Associated Press (AP).[22]

Finally, most stories appearing in newspapers are subjected to multiple editing, often by journalists totally untrained in legal reporting. Naturally this produces a number of distortions in the final copy. Professor Newland has found that most of the stories printed in the newspapers he examined had been edited and offered a great deal of background information and conjecture rather than detailed legal reasoning. Several articles reported incorrect information and often the headlines were misleading. Stories published after decisions were rendered virtually ignored what the Supreme Court decided and focused instead on national, state, and local reactions to the decisions.[23]

Perhaps David Grey has best summarized the role of newspapers in reporting Supreme Court decisions: "There is a general absence of penetrating coverage of long-term trends and legal developments," he concludes, "while much of the short-term news coverage that does exist ends up preoccupied with the drama of the 'new event' or the persons and organizations involved and not enough with the why and the explanation of what it all *really means,* anyhow."[24]

Periodicals

Periodicals are another means by which Supreme Court decisions may be channeled to the public. Included in this category are general periodicals (magazines of general circulation), specialized journals and magazines (occupational publications), and specialized memoranda (bulletins and newsletters). It has been suggested that these materials provide more intensive and detailed coverage than does the daily press.[25] As with radio, television, and newspapers, however, periodicals have serious limitations. The most glaring is that although they "may" carry "reliable" information on Court decisions, most of them do not.

General Periodicals

The most popular magazine of general circulation listed was *Time. Newsweek* was a close second, and *U. S. News and World Report* was a distant third. These periodicals frequently do carry information about Court decisions. Several other magazines of general circulation were mentioned, among them *Atlantic, Business Week, Forbes, Fortune, Harpers, National Observer, National Review, New*

Republic, New Yorker, Playboy, Reader's Digest, Saturday Review, and *The Progressive.* Rarely do these publications carry information about Supreme Court decisions, although a number have sporadically published articles on topics legal in nature.

Specialized Literature

It is clear that members of each group also perceived that they received information from "occupational" magazines.[26] For example, doctors frequently listed medical journals, attorneys and judges listed the law reviews, bar journals, and the opinions themselves, clergy members listed various religious periodicals, and law enforcement officers listed various police magazines and journals.

To test whether these perceptions were accurate, several issues of each publication were examined for the period immediately following important Court decisions directly relevant to each occupational group.[27] Subsequently, each periodical was perused for approximately a two-year period.

Doctors. No specific literature dominated the list of periodicals suggested by the doctors. Most frequently mentioned was the *American Medical Association Journal.* Issues were examined for articles about the abortion decisions of 1973. Not only were none found in these issues, but no articles whatsoever on Court decisions appeared in others that were examined. Only the *Journal of the Florida Medical Association* and the *American Journal of Psychiatry* occasionally carry articles of a legal nature, and, indeed, these are very limited in scope and in substance. Doctors, like clergy members, school board members, lawmakers, and law enforcement officers, suggested that the *Kiplinger Letter* was a channel from which they received information. However, rarely does the *Letter* carry articles on Court decisions.

Attorneys. As one might expect, attorneys most frequently list the *Florida Bar Journal* as a channel of information about U. S. Supreme Court decisions. However, the *Journal* carries almost nothing about such decisions. Indeed, there was not even mention made of the *Argersinger* opinion, a case which had originated within Florida and had vast implications for the entire state. This was true of many of the other journals mentioned. However, unlike the sources listed by other occupational groups (except judges), a majority of the sources cited by attorneys do carry a great deal of information about Supreme Court decisions.

Judges. As with attorneys, judges frequently listed the *Florida Bar Journal* as a channel of communication. The most popular channel, however, was the *American Bar Association Journal,* which does have excellent coverage of recent Supreme Court decisions. A number of judges reported reading *Judicature* for such information. However, this journal has only a limited review of such material.

Clergy Members. Clergy members listed several publications specific to their religious affiliation as carrying information about Supreme Court decisions. However, only two, *Christianity and Crisis* and *The Christian Century,* carried articles on the abortion decisions, and only the latter carried an in-depth, substantive critique of those decisions. *The Christian Century* was also the only magazine to carry articles on the obscenity cases and the death penalty decision.

School Teachers. As with most of the publics, educators listed a number of journals that carry absolutely no articles on Supreme Court decisions. Legally related articles do occasionally appear in the *Florida Education Association Tabloid* and *American Scholar,* but these are brief and do not deal explicitly with Court decisions. On the other hand, *Educational Digest, Phi Delta Kappan,* and *Today's Education* do publish comprehensive articles on the subject. Indeed, each carried in-depth critiques of the 1973 school teachers salary case.

Law Enforcement Officers. As with doctors, no specific literature dominated the list of periodicals suggested by law enforcement officers.[28] Numerous sheriff's deputies, state troopers, and city police officers did list newsletters, departmental memoranda, and bulletins. Indeed, they were the only group to list specific interdepartmental communiqués as a usual channel of information.[29] However, almost none of the channels carry information about the Supreme Court. For example, many listed the Attorney General's newsletter. However, the letter almost exclusively carries information about state decisions.[30] Moreover, most of the occupational magazines they listed do not carry such information. For example, *Florida on Patrol,* the most widely circulated police magazine in the state, did not report the *Papachristou* or *Gustafson* decisions. This is also true of *Florida Police Journal, The Florida Sheriff, Florida Sheriff's Star,* and *Florida Police Chief.* On the other hand, law enforcement officers did occasionally mention the *Journal of Criminal Law, Criminology and Police Science* and *Search and Seizure Bulletin,* both of which carry a great deal of information about the Court's decisions.

Bookstore and Movie Theatre Operators. There were simply too few responses in these categories to draw any conclusions.

School Board Members. The only magazine listed which regularly reports cases is *Nation's Schools.*

Lawmakers. In checking for information about the reapportionment cases, specifically *Baker* v. *Carr* and *Reynolds* v. *Sims,* and a recent vagrancy case,

Papachristou v. *Jacksonville,* it was again found that most of the magazines listed by lawmakers do not carry articles on these locally important Supreme Court decisions. Some general information about the Court can be found in *Cities, Human Events, National Review,* and *Nations.*

Copies of the Decisions

The most obvious means by which Supreme Court decisions may be channeled to the public is via the opinions themselves. The U. S. Government Printing Office prints an official version, and two private companies, the Lawyers Co-Operative Publishing Company and West Publishing Company, print annotated versions. Additionally, a loose-leaf service is provided by the Bureau of National Affairs that reports decisions within a few days of their delivery. The *Criminal Law Reporter* reproduces criminal procedure holdings. A major problem with utilizing opinions as a channel from which to obtain information about Supreme Court decisions is that they are not readily available. Wasby, for example, notes that in rural states such as North Dakota, there may be only a few copies of the *U. S. Reports* in the entire state.[31] In Wyoming, he reports that only Casper, Laramie, and Cheyenne have these publications.[32] In Illinois, he found that over half of the counties reported that no copies were available.

Decisions may be found in law libraries. However, several states have only one or two such libraries, and a few have none. It is true that most state supreme courts retain a collection of decisions, but their availability to the general public is often restricted. The decisions are also usually available in major college and university libraries, but again, such facilities are limited in number, and their accessibility is often limited, even to those in the immediate geographic locale.

Statistical Findings

As mentioned at the beginning of this chapter, each respondent in the survey was asked to state whether or not he usually obtained reliable information about Supreme Court decisions from (1) radio or television, (2) newspapers, (3) general periodicals, (4) specialized memoranda, bulletins, or newsletters, (5) specialized magazines or journals, and/or (6) the opinion itself. Table 5-1 reports the findings.

Of the six channels, newspapers were selected most frequently. Indeed, with only two exceptions, at least three quarters of the membership of each public pointed to this media as a usual conduit. It is interesting to note that the three groups relying least on this channel — judges, attorneys, and law enforcement officers — are the publics whose professions require that they keep abreast of recent decisions. This is perhaps an implicit recognition of the problems

Table 5-1
Channels by Which Various Publics Usually Obtain Reliable Information about Supreme Court Decisions

Occupational Group	Newspapers	TV or Radio	Specialized Memoranda	General Periodicals	Special Journals	Opinion Itself
Doctors (N = 70)	90%	80%	30%	86%	41%	6%
Attorneys (N = 84)	60	51	81	50	87	81
Judges (N = 115)	48	39	74	44	76	87
Clergy Members (N = 62)	89	89	42	77	48	16
School Teachers (N = 104)	91	95	43	83	43	25
Law Officers (N = 497)	75	71	80	48	53	44
Bookstore Operators (N = 30)	90	93	33	83	40	17
Moviehouse Operators (N = 16)	81	88	19	62	31	6
School Board Members (N = 27)	89	85	63	70	41	4
Lawmakers (N = 106)	80	67	61	59	53	35
Total (N = 1111)	76	71	66	58	55	42

surrounding press coverage of Supreme Court decisions discussed earlier in this chapter.

Similarly, although television or radio was relied on to a great extent by most groups, again, a sizeable proportion of these three publics did not perceive either television or radio as a channel from which they usually obtained reliable information. Nor did lawmakers, a group composed of many attorneys.

Specialized memoranda, bulletins, and newsletters were chosen most frequently by law enforcement officers, attorneys, and judges. This is to be expected. Law enforcement officers are organized in a highly bureaucratic manner and employ regularized lines of communication of a paramilitary nature. Public attorneys and judges are likewise members of professions that utilize regularized channels of communication.[33] Moreover, they are highly unified groups that systematically participate in intragroup activities both professionally and socially. On the other hand, the three groups selecting the specialized memoranda channel least frequently, moviehouse operators, doctors, and bookstore operators, are amorphous, highly decentralized groups, which are often widely dispersed geographically as well as socially. As a result, regularized lines of communication are almost nonexistent.

The frequency in selecting general periodicals did not vary greatly from group to group. Again, however, the three groups relying least on this channel were attorneys, judges, and law enforcement officers. Conversely, these publics along with lawmakers, more than any other group, relied on specialized magazines or periodicals for their information about Supreme Court decisions. This fact has great import, for as suggested earlier, only these groups claim to read literature that *actually* carries a substantial amount of information about court decisions.

As is to be expected, the groups most closely dealing with the law on a regular basis were more likely than others to claim that they read the opinions themselves. Doctors, clergy members, bookstore operators, moviehouse operators, and school board members candidly admitted they did not read opinions. Indeed, such literature for the most part may simply be unavailable to them as suggested earlier. However, school teachers present a unique case. Twenty-five percent claimed to have relied on this channel. Most would agree that this appears extremely high.

Conclusions

It should be clear from the foregoing analysis that two categories of publics have emerged. The first is composed of professions intimately connected with the law on a *continuous* basis (attorneys, judges, law enforcement officers, and lawmakers). The second is composed of publics who have only *intermittent* interest in Supreme Court decisions (all others).

Continuous publics have the greatest need for accurate information about Supreme Court decisions. Fortunately they do not rely on the weakest channels to the extent that intermittent publics do. Indeed, they have much less propensity to rely on the broadcast media, which are particularly suspect as a reliable conduit. Moreover, they do not rely as heavily on newspapers as do the others. On the other hand, continuous publics do rely to a much greater extent on channels that regularly provide accurate information about important decisions. Among these are specialized memoranda, bulletins, and newsletters, specialized magazines or journals, and the opinions themselves.

Intermittent publics conversely rely much more heavily on television, radio, and general periodicals. The first two, as we have noted, have serious defects as conduits of information about Supreme Court decisions. Perhaps the most reliable source is the general periodical. Indeed, *Time, Newsweek,* and *U. S. News and World Report* regularly carry such articles as do a number of other periodicals mentioned.

It must be again emphasized that these generalizations are based on perceptions of where respondents believe they usually receive reliable information about the Court and its opinions. It will be recalled that upon perusing the specialized literature suggested by the various publics, most was devoid of such information, thus indicating a great deal of misperception on the part of many.

The quantity and quality of information actually obtained from these channels is the subject of the next two chapters.

Notes

1. Burns W. Roper, *Trends in Attitudes Toward Television and Other Media: A Fourteen Year Review,* (New York: Roper Organization, Television Information Office, 1973), pp. 2-3.

2. Newton Minow, et al., *Presidential Television* (New York: Basic Books, 1973), pp. 100-01.

3. Ibid., pp. 95-96.

4. Everette Dennis, "Another Look At Press Coverage of the Supreme Court," *Villanova Law Review,* 20 (March 1975), 775, n. 49.

5. Ibid., 790-91, n. 119.

6. For a discussion of the problem of noise see David Berlo, *The Process of Communication* (New York: Holt, Rinehart and Winston, 1960), pp. 40-41.

7. David L. Grey, *The Supreme Court and the News Media* (Evanston, Ill.: Northwestern University, 1968), p. 129.

8. Neal Milner, *The Court and Local Law Enforcement* (Beverly Hills, Cal.: Sage Publications, 1971), pp. 92, 118, 142, 172.

9. Quoted in, Mark Cannon, "An Administrator's View of the Supreme Court," *Federal Bar News,* 22 (April 1975), 112.

10. Dennis, *supra* note 4, at 790, n. 119.

11. Chester Newland, "Press Coverage of the United States Supreme Court," *Western Political Quarterly*, 17 (March 1964), 16-17. See also Dennis, *supra* note 4, at 765.

12. Newland, *supra* note 11, at 17-18.

13. Dennis, *supra* note 4, at 791.

14. For a detailed account of one reporter's activities see David Grey, "Decision-Making by a Reporter Under Deadline Pressure," *Journalism Quarterly*, 43 (Autumn 1966), 419-28.

15. Anthony Lewis, "Problems of a Washington Correspondent," *Connecticut Bar Journal*, 33 (December 1959), 365.

16. Lionel Sobel, "News Coverage of the Supreme Court," *American Bar Association Journal*, 56 (June 1970), 548.

17. John MacKenzie, "The Warren Court and the Press," *Michigan Law Review*, 67 (December 1968), 306.

18. Stephen Wasby, *The Impact of the United States Supreme Court* (Homewood, Ill.: The Dorsey Press, 1970), p. 95. Wasby points out elsewhere that "certiorari denials are mistaken for full opinions of the Court." Stephen Wasby, "How to Get an Idea from Here to There: The Court and Communication Overload," *Public Affairs Bulletin*, 3 (November-December 1970), p. 1. See also Irving Kaufman, "The Courts and the Public: A Problem in Communication," *American Bar Association Journal*, 54 (December 1968), 1192-93; and "On Covering the Court," *Columbia Journalism Review*, 1 (Fall 1962), 2. The Dennis study informs us that five of twenty-four reporters covering the Supreme Court in 1974 were able to point to an example of inaccurate reporting by their colleagues. Dennis, *supra* note 4, at 794.

19. Daniel Berman, *It Is So Ordered* (New York: W. W. Norton and Company, 1966), p. vii.

20. Newland, *supra* note 11, at 20.

21. Dennis, *supra* note 4, at 790, n. 119. He also reports semiregular coverage by the *Wall Street Journal, Los Angeles Times, Boston Globe* and *Baltimore Sun*.

22. Dennis, *supra* note 4, at 774, n. 46.

23. Newland, *supra* note 11, at 31-32.

24. Grey, *supra* note 7, p. 120.

25. Wasby, *The Impact of the U. S. Supreme Court*, *supra* note 18, p. 88.

26. See Appendix B for a list of the specialized periodicals chosen by each group.

27. The selections were as follows: **Doctors:** Doe v. Bolton, 410 U. S. 179 (1973); and Roe v. Wade, 410 U. S. 113 (1973). **Attorneys:** Gustafson v. Florida, 414 U. S. 260 (1973); United States v. Robinson, 414 U. S. 218 (1973); and Argersinger v. Hamlin, 407 U. S. 25 (1972). **Judges:** Argersinger v. Hamlin, 407 U. S. 25 (1972); and Williams v. Florida, 399 U. S. 78 (1970). **Clergy:** Doe

v. Bolton, 410 U. S. 179 (1973); Roe v. Wade, 410 U. S. 113 (1973); and Griswold v. Connecticut, 381 U. S. 479 (1965). **Teachers:** Tilton v. Richardson, 403 U. S. 672 (1971); Lemon v. Kurtzman, 403 U. S. 602 (1971); Abington School District v. Schempp, 374 U. S. 203 (1963); and Murray v. Curlett, 374 U. S. 179 (1963). **Law Officers:** Gustafson v. Florida, 414 U. S. 260 (1973); United States v. Robinson, 414 U. S. 218 (1973); and Papachristou v. City of Jacksonville, 405 U. S. 156 (1972). **Bookstore and Movie Operators:** Paris Adult Theater v. Slaton, 413 U. S. 49 (1973); and Miller v. California, 413 U. S. 1 (1973). **School Board Members:** Same as teachers. **Lawmakers:** Papachristou v. City of Jacksonville, 405 U. S. 156 (1972); Reynolds v. Sims, 377 U. S. 533 (1964); and Baker v. Carr, 369 U. S. 186 (1962).

28. Stephen Wasby listed the channels that law enforcement officers might possibly utilize. See "From Supreme Court to Policemen: A Partial Inventory of Materials," *Criminal Law Bulletin,* 8 (September 1972), 587-615.

29. This is obviously due in part to the hierarchical nature of such departments.

30. Newsletters are beginning to play a more important role. For example, Wasby notes that "A number of attorney's general are initiating programs by which summaries of, and commentaries upon, Supreme Court decisions of relevance to law enforcement officers are regularly sent to the latter, by means of a series of 'newsletters' or memoranda." Wasby, *The Impact of the United States Supreme Court, supra* note 18, p. 90. These are not to be confused with opinions of the attorneys general. Further, some district attorneys are doing the same thing.

31. Stephen Wasby, "Police and the Law in Illinois: A First Look at the Communication of Supreme Court Decisions," *Public Affairs Bulletin,* 5 (September-October 1972), 4.

32. Stephen Wasby, "The Communication of the Supreme Court's Criminal Procedure Decisions: A Preliminary Mapping," *Villanova Law Review,* 18 (June 1973), 1090.

33. The phrase "public attorney" is used here to emphasize that only sixteen private attorneys responded to the questionnaire. Thus, respondents in this category are overwhelmingly state employees.

6

The Decoders: Public Elites

The two-step flow of communication theory developed by Katz and Lazarsfeld suggests that there are two separable groups of message targets: public elites (henceforth decoders) and public subordinates. The former is the subject of the present chapter.

Each respondent to the survey was asked to select individuals from whom he usually obtains reliable information about Supreme Court decisions. Among the choices were work-related personnel, attorneys (including judges), instructors, and friends. Table 6-1 summarizes the findings. It is clear that the various occupational groups perceive that they acquire information from different sets of decoders.[1]

Work-related Personnel as Decoders

The study by Robert Hodge, et al. referred to in Chapter 3 established a hierarchical ranking of occupations according to their prestige.[2] Doctors were ranked highest, followed by judges, clergy members, attorneys, teachers, and law enforcement officers. A similar scale results when ranking the occupational groups by propensity to reject a boss or superior as a decoder of information. In other words, there is an inverse relationship between a group's prestige rank and the likelihood that its members will rely on superiors for information about Court decisions. For example, doctors claim that they almost never rely on supervisors for such information, whereas law enforcement officers have a great propensity to do so. Indeed, the latter is the only group in which over 50 percent of its membership perceived a boss or superior as a usual decoder of reliable information.

With the exception of law enforcement officers, the members of each group had a greater propensity to select coworkers over superiors or subordinates as usual decoders. Moreover, coworkers were selected at a greater rate by doctors, attorneys, and teachers more often than any other decoder.[3] They were also selected relatively frequently by clergy members. In police departments, on the other hand, law enforcement personnel regularly selected superiors as decoders of information. These facts strongly suggest that in professional organizations, the two-step flow of communication may be horizontal in nature, whereas in desk-class bureaucracies, it is more likely to be vertical.[4]

Table 6-1
Usual Decoders of Reliable Information about Supreme Court Decisions

Occupational Group	Work-related Personnel			Attorneys			Miscellaneous Individuals		
	Coworker	Boss or Superior	Subordinate	Member DA's Office	Member PD's Office	Member AG's Office	Local Judge	Instructor	Friend
Doctors (N = 70)	10%	4%	4%	3%	3%	4%	4%	7%	6%
Attorneys (N = 84)	60	29	34	42	43	36	32	44	8
Judges (N = 115)	30	8	4	40	39	30	40	58	4
Clergy Members (N = 62)	16	11	8	6	6	10	24	21	16
School Teachers (N = 104)	31	24	5	12	14	16	14	12	21
Law Officers (N = 497)	38	62	19	61	27	61	38	60	5
Lawmakers (N = 106)	24	4	13	20	15	42	34	26	4

Attorneys as Decoders

Attorneys by virtue of their training and legal expertise are generally regarded as decoders of Supreme Court decisions. For example, Wasby has noted that decisions of the Court "may come to the attention of a judge only by being cited by a lawyer arguing a case before him. While some judges may regularly follow what the Supreme Court does, others may wait until attorneys bring matters to their attention."[5] Moreover, he continues, "if attorneys do not cite the cases because 'they' are unaware of them, the judge may never hear of them."[6] Thus Wasby has been able to conclude elsewhere that "lawyers may be a more important link in the communications process than is the formal structure of the court system."[7]

Judges are not the only group that may benefit from attorney decoders. To again quote Wasby, "Lawyers also serve as important means of communication by helping to transmit decisions to other attorneys."[8] Additionally, it is equally apparent that attorneys serve as decoders for the public at large. William Muir's portrayal of a lawyer's key role in communicating the Supreme Court's decision in *Schempp* is a case in point.[9] Indeed, the attorney involved was apparently responsible for the resultant high degree of compliance with that decision.

Two occupational groups in the survey are composed primarily, if not exclusively, of lawyers: attorneys and judges. Legislators are also often lawyers. It is interesting to note that these groups consistently chose members of the legal profession (members of the district attorney's office, public defender's office, attorney general's office, and local judge) as decoders at greater rates than did all other occupational groups (except law enforcement officers). On the other hand, doctors and teachers rarely perceived attorneys as their decoders.

Unexpectedly, clergy members most often selected local judges as their decoders. However, they did select coworkers and friends at relatively frequent rates when compared to the other sets of decoders.

Legislators had a greater propensity to claim that they rely primarily on members of the attorney general's office than on other members of the legal profession. This is probably due to the fact that they have ready access to this office while the legislature is in session.

As suggested, the only group not composed primarily of lawyers that selected attorneys as decoders at relatively high rates was law enforcement officers. This is readily understandable when one considers the fact that many of these personnel come into contact weekly, if not daily, with members of the legal profession.

Miscellaneous Individuals as Decoders

Prior studies investigating the utility of instructors as decoders in training sessions and conferences are limited to one occupational group, law enforcement officers.

Neal Milner found that police officers in four large Wisconsin cities, Green Bay, Kenosha, Madison, and Racine, selected instructors at conferences and training sessions as their *best* decoder of information about the *Miranda* decision.[10] In a similar study utilizing essentially the same instrument in small Wisconsin communities, this investigator found that not only were instructors chosen as the *best* decoders of information, but they were also the *preferred* means of learning about Supreme Court decisions.[11]

In the present study instructors again were selected relatively frequently. Indeed, these decoders were selected most often by judges.[12] Instructors were also selected frequently by doctors, lawyers, clergy members, and law enforcement officers.

Friends are generally not perceived as usual decoders of reliable information. In fact, only clergy members and school teachers perceived them as decoders with any degree of frequency.

An In-depth Look at Law Enforcement Officers

To more closely test the extent to which elites serve as decoders of information, law enforcement officers—members of rigidly hierarchical organizations—were examined in detail. The two-step flow of communication theory suggests that: (1) superiors are unlikely to obtain information from subordinates; (2) subordinates are likely to receive information from superiors; (3) superiors are more likely to be aware of Supreme Court decisionmaking areas than are subordinates; and (4) superiors are more likely to possess more accurate information about Supreme Court decisions than are subordinates. It is to these considerations that we now turn.

Propositions I and II

Neal Milner's work in four Wisconsin cities suggests that the first two propositions are correct. Indeed, only in Kenosha did he find that a superior officer selected a subordinate (patrolman) as a first decoder of information about *Miranda.*[13] In no city did a superior choose a subordinate as a best decoder of information.[14] Conversely, in each city subordinates frequently chose superiors as first and best decoders of information. Only in Kenosha did a subordinate select a subordinate. Thus, Milner's data would indicate a confirmation of the first two hypotheses.

The propositions were again tested in the present research. Law enforcement officers were asked: "From which decoders do you usually obtain reliable information about decisions of the United States Supreme Court?" The results are compiled in Table 6-2. The earlier finding that in police departments the

Table 6-2

**Decoders from Whom Law Enforcement Officers Usually Obtain Reliable
Information about Supreme Court Decisions**

Occupational Group	Decoders		
	Superior	*Coworker*	*Subordinate*
Superiors:			
Police Chief (N = 57)	26%	16%	18%
City Captain or Lieutenant (N = 29)	48	35	17
County Sheriff (N = 29)	17	31	21
County Captain or Lieutenant (N = 13)	62	39	15
State Police Officer, Sergeant, or above (N = 42)	55	24	12
Subordinates:			
City Patrolman (N = 114)	81	50	25
County Deputy or Sergeant (N = 83)	74	34	18
State Trooper (I or II) or Corporal (N = 128)	70	48	16

personnel utilize bosses or superiors as conduits of information is verified (see
Table 6-1). Naturally the percentages are low for police chiefs and county
sheriffs because they have few superiors. On the other hand, city police captains
and lieutenants and state police officers do have superiors from whom they may
obtain information. Over 48 percent of each group claimed to utilize such
decoders.

Subordinates overwhelmingly claim that they usually obtain reliable informa
tion about Supreme Court decisions from superiors. Indeed, in each category
over 70 percent of the respondents selected this response. On the other hand,
few city patrolmen, county deputies, or state troopers claim to receive information from subordinates. After all, many of them do not have subordinates.

What is striking is the relative importance of coworkers as decoders of information. Large numbers of subordinates selected these personnel as did a
substantial number of superiors. Again, this seems to indicate that the two-step
flow of communication is at least partially horizontal in nature rather than
entirely vertical.

Proposition III

To test the third proposition, that superiors are more likely to be aware of
Supreme Court decisionmaking areas than are subordinates, law enforcement

officers were asked whether or not the Court had issued decisions in each of twenty-four areas. Table 6-3 summarizes the findings. In fourteen of the areas, subordinates were aware of decisions at higher rates than superiors. Further, in those instances where the superiors were more often aware, the subordinates were not far behind. In the three control areas (flood damage, fire control, smoking), subordinates were much more likely to be correctly aware than were superiors.

The nine areas most directly relevant to law enforcement officials were singled out for special consideration.[15] The mean number of "correctly aware" answers offered by superiors was 7.418, while the mean number for subordinates was 7.382. These findings indicate that there is no significant difference in levels of awareness between superiors and subordinates in police-related decision-making areas.

Table 6-3
Percentage of Law Enforcement Officers Correctly Aware of Areas in Which the Supreme Court Has Recently Delivered Opinions

Area	Superior[a]	Subordinate[b]
Flood Damage	11%	27%
Right to Counsel	95	96
Obscene Movies	91	93
Juvenile Rights	89	91
Abortions	79	82
Drug Offenses	75	78
Wiretapping	95	96
Stop and Frisk	94	97
Fire Control	15	27
Vagrancy	79	76
Trial by Jury	86	81
Death Penalty	95	95
Lord's Prayer	95	96
Drunk Driving	43	41
Smoking	32	39
Bible Reading	89	88
Police Lineups	79	71
Reapportionment	72	52
Taxing Religious Organizations	47	47
Dissemination of Birth Control Information	34	32
Double Jeopardy	63	71
State Aid to Parochial Schools	58	53
Right to Remain Silent	92	92
Obscene Books	89	88

[a]($N = 325$)
[b]($N = 170$)

The same procedure was utilized in the fifteen areas not directly related to law enforcement.[16] The mean for superiors was 9.559 and 9.686 for subordinates, again indicating little difference in the levels of awareness.

Proposition IV

To test the levels of substantive knowledge retained by superiors vis-a-vis subordinates, the two groups were asked specific questions about five recent Supreme Court decisions directly pertinent to law enforcement and one Court decision of general importance to the public at large. Table 6-4 summarizes the responses. In all six categories subordinates were more often correct than superiors. Moreover, subordinates tended to be incorrect less often than superiors. On the other hand, superiors were "unsure" at greater rates than subordinates.

Summary

Propositions I and II are confirmed. Superiors rarely obtain information from subordinates, and the latter often receive information from superiors. However, a strong caveat must be noted. The role of the coworker as a decoder cannot be overemphasized. Indeed, this study reveals a more important role in the communications process for the coworker than has heretofore been recognized.

Propositions III and IV are not confirmed. Indeed, subordinates are more often aware of Supreme Court decisionmaking areas and retain greater levels of substantive knowledge about specific decisions than do superiors.

Conclusions

It is clear that the various occupational groups perceive that they receive information about Supreme Court decisions from a wide variety of decoders. Most, however, rely on work-related personnel. It is equally clear that the dominant perception among members of professions is that they more often receive information about Supreme Court decisions from coworkers than from superiors, subordinates, or extra occupational personnel (see Table 6-1). On the other hand, members of bureaucratic structures, most notably law enforcement officers, perceive that superiors in their hierarchy serve as decoders of decisions. Upon close examination, however, it is found that subordinates possess greater degrees of awareness and greater degrees of substantive information about the Court than do their superiors. Thus, the credibility and reliability of the latter as decoders of information is questionable.

There are other reasons why relying on superiors for such information is

Table 6-4
Law Enforcement Officers' Knowledge about Specific Supreme Court Decisions

Cases	Correct Answers		Incorrect Answers		Unsure	
	Superior	*Subordinate*	*Superior*	*Subordinate*	*Superior*	*Subordinate*
In re Gault, 387 U. S. 1 (1967)	(161) 95%	(308) 97%	(1) 1%	(5) 2%	(7) 4%	(6) 2%
Rochin v. California, 342 U. S. 165 (1952)	(68) 41	(146) 47	(41) 25	(96) 31	(56) 34	(71) 23
Breithaupt v. Abram, 352 U. S. 432 (1957)	(146) 86	(287) 90	(15) 9	(27) 9	(8) 5	(4) 1
United States v. Wade, 388 U. S. 218 (1967)	(147) 87	(276) 87	(8) 5	(12) 4	(14) 8	(30) 9
Terry v. Ohio, 392 U. S. 1 (1968)	(147) 88	(282) 89	(16) 10	(35) 11	(4) 2	(1) 0
Oregon v. Mitchell, 400 U. S. 112 (1970)	(23) 14	(91) 29	(114) 69	(175) 55	(29) 18	(51) 16

hazardous. In the first place, it should be pointed out that the degree of receptivity by elites to a particular decision may influence the accuracy and speed with which the message is transmitted. If elites are "hard on crime," for example, opinions adverse to the police may be conveyed much more slowly and less accurately than favorable decisions. If, on the other hand, the opinion coincides with the existing social milieu, political culture, and belief systems of the elites, there may be a much greater chance that the communication will take place with a high degree of accuracy.

Finally, many groups are not organized in bureaucratic fashion, and therefore they lack an ongoing hierarchy through which messages may be transmitted. Doctors and judges, for example, are members of professions that generally deemphasize superior-subordinate relationships. Indeed, there is often a total absence of such relationships, and thus there may be no superior available to decode information.

Notes

1. Moviehouse operators, bookstore operators and school board members are omitted from the following analysis due to the relatively low numbers of responses within those categories.

2. Robert Hodge, et al., "Occupational Prestige in the United States, 1925-63," *American Journal of Sociology,* 70 (November 1964), 290-92.

3. Bookstore operators also choose coworkers with greater propensity than any other group of decoders.

4. See Victor Thompson, *Bureaucracy and Modern World* (Morristown, N. J.: General Learning Press, 1976), p. 33.

5. Stephen Wasby, "The Communication of the Supreme Court's Criminal Procedure Decisions: A Preliminary Mapping," *Villanova Law Review,* 18 (June 1973), 1091.

6. Ibid.

7. Stephen Wasby, "Police and the Law in Illinois: A First Look at the Communication of Supreme Court Decisions," *Public Affairs Bulletin,* 5 (September-October 1972), 2.

8. Wasby, *supra* note 5, at 1092.

9. William Muir, *Law and Attitude Change* (Chicago: University of Chicago Press, 1973), pp. 17-20.

10. Neal Milner, *The Court and Local Law Enforcement* (Beverly Hills, Cal.: Sage Publications, 1971), pp. 96, 121, 146, 177.

11. Larry Berkson, "The United States Supreme Court and Small-Town Police Officers: A Study in Communication," (Unpublished manuscript, 1970).

12. School board members also chose this decoder most often.

13. Milner, *supra* note 10, p. 118.

14. Ibid., pp. 92, 96, 118, 121, 142, 146, 172, 177.

15. Right to counsel, juvenile rights, drug offenses, wiretapping, stop and frisk, vagrancy, drunk driving, police lineups, and the right to remain silent.

16. Flood damage, obscene movies, abortions, fire control, trial by jury, death penalty, Lord's Prayer in school, smoking, Bible reading in school, re-apportionment, taxing religious organizations, dissemination of birth control information, double jeopardy, state aid to parochial schools, and obscene literature.

7 The Receivers: The Public

The ultimate test of any communications system is the amount of substantive information obtained by receivers about the message being transmitted. In fact, as David Berlo has written, "If the source does not reach the receiver with his message, he might as well have talked to himself."[1] It is to this subject that we now turn.

It must be reemphasized at the outset that the respondents to the survey should be expected to possess comparatively high levels of information about Supreme Court decisions. First, as was noted in Chapter 1, the sample is very elite in nature. There are no pretenses that it represents a cross-section of the population. Second, for purposes of this study, all 1111 respondents were considered target publics, and thus no attempt was made to segregate decoders from receivers. Such an approach appears justifiable on the grounds that a judicial mandate is as much directed toward superiors as to subordinates in American democratic society. Third, with one notable exception, the respondents were asked only about decisions directly relating to their occupations. In most instances the cases inquired about could or should be applied on a regular basis by the receiver.

Substantive Knowledge

Table 7-1 summarizes the responses, by occupational group, to specific questions about Supreme Court decisions. Discounting the groups that were asked only one or two questions, law enforcement officers ranked first in the average percentage of correct responses (80 percent). Only two other groups exceeded the fiftieth percentile: judges (64 percent) and attorneys (58 percent). The average percentage of correct responses for the remaining groups is as follows: lawmakers (34 percent), clergy members (26 percent), school teachers (26 percent), and school board members (25 percent).

Law Enforcement Officers

It is readily apparent that law enforcement officers retain relatively high levels of knowledge about occupationally related Supreme Court decisions. They possess extensive knowledge about juvenile rights (to remain silent and have an attorney present during a hearing), the involuntary extraction of a blood

Table 7-1
Responses to Specific Questions about Supreme Court Decisions[a]

Occupational Group	Question Area[b]	Percent Correct	Percent Incorrect	Percent Unsure
Doctors	Pumping of Stomach	57.1	2.9	34.3
(N = 70)	Extracting Blood	37.1	37.1	17.1
Attorneys	Right to Jury Trial	79.8	4.8	10.7
(N = 84)	Death Penalty	35.7	35.7	19.0
	Double Jeopardy	25.0	60.7	9.5
	Admissibility of Testimony	85.7	3.6	3.6
	Attorney at Lineup	61.9	19.0	8.3
Judges	Juvenile Rights	94.8	0.9	2.6
(N = 115)	Death Penalty	47.8	29.6	13.0
	Double Jeopardy	20.9	63.5	10.4
	Admissibility of Testimony	74.8	11.3	7.0
	Attorney at Lineup	82.6	5.2	6.1
Clergy Members	State-written Prayers	29.0	45.2	21.0
(N = 62)	Bible Reading	40.3	33.9	21.0
	Recitation of Lord's Prayer	24.2	58.1	14.5
School	State-written Prayers	17.3	61.5	16.3
Teachers	Bible Reading	26.0	54.8	13.5
(N = 104)	Financing School Systems	44.2	30.8	18.3
	Recitation of Lord's Prayer	17.3	65.4	13.5
Law Officers	Juvenile Rights	94.8	1.2	2.6
(N = 497)	Pumping of Stomach	43.1	27.8	25.6
	Extracting Blood	87.5	8.5	2.4
	Attorney at Lineup	85.5	4.0	8.9
	Stop and Frisk	86.7	10.3	1.0
Bookstore Operators (N = 30)	"Contemporary Community Standards"	66.7	6.7	23.3
Moviehouse Operators (N = 16)	"Contemporary Community Standards"	81.3	6.3	12.5
School Board	State-written Prayers	7.4	63.0	22.2
Members	Bible Reading	25.9	51.9	14.8
(N = 27)	Financing School Systems	40.7	51.9	3.7
	Recitation of Lord's Prayer	25.9	51.9	11.1
Lawmakers	Censorship of Movies	39.6	41.5	12.3
(N = 106)	Recitation of Lord's Prayer	60.4	26.4	7.5
	Prohibition of Abortions	33.1	53.8	10.4
	Financing School Systems	28.3	50.9	14.2
	Death Penalty	44.3	33.0	16.0

[a]Percentages do not total 100 percent because of a few "no responses."
[b]The questions are found in Appendix C.

sample to determine sobriety, the right to counsel during a lineup (if it is a critical stage in the judicial process), and the right of police officers to stop and frisk suspicious-looking persons. Strangely, however, over 10 percent of the respondents were incorrect about the latter.

The question presenting the greatest difficulty for law enforcement officers involved the involuntary pumping of a person's stomach to retrieve, as evidence, narcotic pills that have been recently swallowed. Only 43 percent correctly answered the question. Twenty-eight percent responded incorrectly, while 26 percent were unsure. This is readily explainable. The case in point is the oldest of the group, having been rendered by the Court in 1952.[2] Secondly, there are only rare instances when the case can be applied. Indeed, few police officers encounter such a situation during their entire careers.

Judges

As a group, judges were very knowledgeable about the rights of juveniles and the right of defendants to retain attorneys at lineup. Nearly three-fourths were cognizant of the fact that testimony, inadmissible as part of the prosecution's case under *Miranda*,[3] could be used to impeach a defendant's credibility.[4]

Judges proved to be considerably less knowledgeable in other areas, however. Over half, for example, did not comprehend the basic thrust of the death penalty decision.[5] In part, this may be due to the fact that the survey question could be variously interpreted. A better explanation, however, is that the "new" Florida statute providing for the death penalty allows the very thing that *Furman* sought to limit: unbridled discretion on the part of judge and jury. The statute provides for a verdict of guilt or innocence at an initial trial and a separate determination of sentence at a second.[6] In the latter proceeding, juries receive evidence of mitigating and aggravating circumstances and *recommend* to the judge whether life imprisonment or the death penalty should be imposed. The recommendation may be unanimous or split. Nonetheless, a judge is free to reject the suggestion, and a few have done so on occasion. It is understandable that one working within such a system might believe *wide* discretion in imposing the death penalty is constitutionally permissible.[7]

Oddly enough, the question that an overwhelming number of judges failed to answer correctly involved a double jeopardy case originating in Florida. Involved was a militant black leader who had gained wide publicity throughout the state for his protest activities. The judges were asked whether a defendant who had been convicted of violating a city ordinance could be convicted of a similar state statute using the same evidence. Just three years before the survey was conducted, the Supreme Court had held that such a practice violated the fifth and fourteenth amendments.[8]

Attorneys

The level of information acquired by attorneys in three of the five areas is surprisingly low. Like judges, they were very familiar with the fact that testimony inadmissible as part of the prosecution's case under *Miranda* may be used to impeach a defendant's credibility. They were also highly cognizant of the fact that a defendant has the right to a jury trial in nonpetty cases. At the other extreme were the low levels of knowledge about the death penalty decision and the double jeopardy case. With regard to the former, it should be noted that 19 percent were unsure about the answer. Nearly 61 percent of the attorneys responded incorrectly to the latter. During interviews with both judges and attorneys, it became apparent that they simply were unfamiliar with the double jeopardy case. Perhaps this is attributable to the fact that the decision is limited in scope and rarely does either group have occasion to utilize it.

Only 62 percent of the attorneys realized that defendants have the right to an attorney at lineup. This frequency is much lower than that of judges and law enforcement officers. Moreover, 19 percent of the attorneys answered incorrectly. Why this is so is not readily apparent. One partial explanation is that some of the private attorneys responding to the survey may have been involved in essentially civil rather than criminal practice.

Lawmakers

Of the five questions asked lawmakers, the only one answered correctly with any degree of frequency involved the recitation of the Lord's Prayer in public schools (60 percent). On the other hand, over a quarter of the respondents believed the practice constitutionally permissible. Nearly 50 percent were correct about the death penalty decision. However, only 40 percent of the sample realized that lawmakers have the right to censor obscene movies, and only 33 percent were cognizant of the fact that lawmakers do not have the right to prohibit abortions during the first three months of pregnancy. They were also relatively unaware of the *Rodriguez* decision.[9] When asked whether lawmakers have the right to finance school systems using a property tax scheme that ultimately allows one district to spend $356 per pupil and another to spend $594 per pupil, only 28 percent answered correctly that it is permissible. Fifty-one percent were incorrect.

It is surprising that lawmakers are not better acquainted with the decisions in the latter three areas. The cases were recently decided, and all three represent areas in which there has been a substantial amount of public controversy. Indeed, in the "Bible Belt" region, there has been very strong opposition to abortion decisions.[10]

Clergy Members

Clergy members were asked three questions about recent Court holdings. It is readily apparent that their levels of knowledge are very low. Only 40 percent appreciated the fact that it is unconstitutional to allow Bible reading in public schools. A mere 29 percent understood that lawmakers are not allowed to write a prayer for morning exercises, and only 24 percent realized that reciting the Lord's Prayer in public schools is unconstitutional. Moreover, clergy members had the second highest average of "percent unsure" responses. Thus it appears that they are relatively unknowledgeable about the substance of important Court decisions.

School Teachers

An overwhelming majority of school teachers were ignorant of the fact that it is unconstitutional to allow both Bible reading and recitation of the Lord's Prayer in public schools. Moreover, nearly 62 percent believed that it is permissible for a teacher to write a prayer for morning exercises. This fact is particularly important because very few of the respondents were teaching in private schools.[11] There are two possible explanations for the large number of incorrect answers. First, some of the respondents are undoubtedly strong opponents of the decision.[12] Thus, an attempt is made to evade it by distinguishing between their practice and the Court's decision. For example, one respondent believed that it is permissible for a teacher to write a prayer for morning exercises, but that he or she "cannot enforce listening." Second, there has been little direction from the local school board. Seventy-eight percent of the respondents taught in one public school system. Upon interviewing a number of officials affiliated with the county board, it is clear that there is no discernible policy stating what a teacher may or may not do during morning exercises. Indeed, there is great ambiguity about what the policy should be. The system in this respect is entirely decentralized and it remains with individual teachers to exercise their discretion. This has resulted in broad noncompliance with the Court's decisions.

Oddly, a much larger percentage of the teachers were knowledgeable about financing school systems. This may be explained by the fact that the decision relating to this subject had only recently been delivered and that it had received a great number of comments in the local media.

School Board Members

As with the school teachers, school board members were relatively unknowledgeable about the school prayer decision. And again, over 62 percent believed that state-written prayers can be permissibly recited in public schools. Apparently, either these decisions have not flowed through the communications system, or the receivers have simply blocked them from their consciousness because of their vehement opposition to them.

Doctors, Moviehouse Operators, and Bookstore Operators

Only two questions were asked of doctors. Over half were cognizant of the fact that it is not permissible to pump a person's stomach to retrieve evidence that has been recently swallowed. A very large portion of this group reported that they were "unsure" about this procedure, whereas only 3 percent were incorrect. A somewhat smaller percentage of doctors realized that it was constitutionally permissible to take a blood sample to determine one's sobriety.

Moviehouse and bookstore operators were asked only one question: What geographic area is utilized to determine "Contemporary Community Standards"? Eighty-one percent of the former and 67 percent of the latter correctly chose "local" over "national" standards.

To further test the levels of substantive knowledge retained by the receivers, they were asked to describe an opinion directly relevant to their occupation. Table 7-2 presents the mixed results. Few respondents could clearly describe the case in question. Only judges responded correctly more than 40 percent of the time. It appears almost unbelievable that only 22.9 percent of the doctors could clearly describe the abortion decisions and that only 22.6 percent of the attorneys could do so for the *Argersinger* decision. Perhaps of greatest import is that only 12.5 percent of the school teachers clearly stated the requirements of the school prayer decisions. If one assumes that a vast majority of the "percent missing" column actually represents "I don't know" responses, the percentage of each occupational group not comprehending the decision is remarkably high.

On the other hand, if the clearly correct and partially correct columns are combined, some occupational groups reflect a relatively high degree of substantive knowledge about Supreme Court decisions. This is especially true in the case of doctors where the percentage reaches 72.9. The large number of partially correct answers is probably due to the complexity of the decisions involved. Two other groups, judges and clergy members, reflect a relatively high degree of knowledge about decisions (69.6 percent and 62.9 percent respectively).

They are followed by law enforcement officers (45.9 percent), school board members (40.7 percent), lawmakers (35.9 percent), school teachers (34.6 percent), moviehouse operators (25.1 percent), and bookstore operators (20

Table 7-2
Explanations of Supreme Court Decisions

Occupational Group	Case	Percent Clearly Correct	Percent Partially Correct	Percent Incorrect	Percent Missing[a]
Doctors (N = 70)	Abortion	23	50	6	21
Attorneys (N = 84)	Right to Counsel	23	14	6	54
Judges (N = 105)	Right to Counsel	43	27	4	26
Clergy Members (N = 62)	Abortion	36	27	8	29
School Teachers (N = 104)	Prayers in Public Schools	13	22	13	53
Law Officers (N = 497)	Vagrancy	37	9	2	52
Bookstore Operators (N = 30)	Obscene Movies	13	7	10	70
Moviehouse Operators (N = 16)	Obscene Movies	6	19	25	50
School Board Members (N = 27)	Prayers in Public Schools	0	41	15	44
Lawmakers (N = 106)	Reapportionment	26	10	6	58

[a]Includes unintelligible answers, answers of unsure and unknown, plus unrecorded answers.

percent). These figures, although somewhat low for the latter groups, are still clearly higher than those found for the general population.

As a final check on the level of substantive knowledge retained by the respondents, an identical question was placed on each of the questionnaires. Contrary to the questions previously mentioned, it was not specifically relevant to any one group. Rather, it was based on a decision having broad implications for all members of society. Each respondent was asked whether or not it is constitutionally permissible for a state to prohibit persons from voting for the president or vice-president until they have resided within the state for six months.[13] Table 7-3 reports the results.

Table 7-3

Knowledge about Residency Requirements for Voting[a]

Occupational Group	Percent Correct	Percent Incorrect	Percent Unsure
Doctors (N = 70)	14	60	21
Attorneys (N = 84)	14	68	16
Judges (N = 115)	5	84	4
Clergy Members (N = 62)	23	61	13
School Teachers (N = 104)	31	57	9
Law Officers (N = 497)	23	59	16
Bookstore Operators (N = 30)	27	57	17
Moviehouse Operators (N = 16)	38	38	25
School Board Members (N = 27)	33	52	7
Lawmakers (N = 106)	8	83	4
Combined	20	64	13

[a]Percentages do not total 100 percent because of a few "no responses."

Surprisingly, moviehouse operators, school board members, and school teachers ranked highest. Follow-up interviews with several members of each category, however, indicated that many of the respondents simply guessed at the answer to this fixed alternative question.

Perhaps most revealing about the table is that very few lawmakers correctly answered the question. The *Dunn* decision, after all, most closely affected this group. Indeed, it nullified their authority to enact legislation establishing such a residency requirement. Also notable are the relatively low correct response rates by judges and attorneys, members of professions who must constantly pay attention to Supreme Court decisions.

Conclusions

At the beginning of this chapter it was hypothesized that the respondents would possess a relatively high level of information about Court decisions. In part this has been borne out. Although no data exist with which to compare the findings, few would argue that the percentages of correct responses found in Table 7-1 and the clearly and partially correct answers found in Table 7-2 are representative of the population at large. Indeed, the number of correct responses in several categories is exceedingly high.

Despite the relatively high levels of substantive knowledge about Court decisions, a large number of individuals simply were incorrect or unsure about many of the decisions that affect their occupational lives. In many instances this is crucial. The fact that judges may not be cognizant of juvenile rights, rules controlling the admissibility of testimony, and the right of defendants to retain an attorney at lineup has the dire prospect of depriving an individual of his constitutional rights. This dearth of knowledge also has the effect of causing the state (society) to incur great expenses in time and money for unnecessary appeals taken to reverse incorrect decisions rendered at the trial level. Similarly, a law enforcement officer may deprive a juvenile or adult of many rights because of his lack of knowledge about Court decisions. Conversely, society is deprived of an efficient and effective police force if officers are unaware that they may perform a "stop and frisk" on suspicious-looking persons after complying with certain procedural requirements.

The nonoccupationally related question about residency requirements for voting reflects a very low level of general substantive knowledge (see Table 7-3) and follow-up interviews indicated that even these levels were probably inflated by a high rate of successful guesses. Lack of knowledge about such a subject may not be crucial. It may not mean life or death as is often the case with doctors vis-a-vis the abortion decisions, or judges vis-a-vis the death penalty decision. Nonetheless, one might argue that in the least, legislators should be knowledgeable about the decision. It might be further argued that many elites should be cognizant of such decisions if for no other reason than to promote the tenets of good citizenship and fundamental concepts associated with representative democracy.

As was suggested in Chapter 1, research on the impact of U. S. Supreme Court decisions suggests that not all local officials execute the specific edicts of the Court. Indeed, several scholars have found a great deal of noncompliance with such decisions. The implication in most of these studies is that such inaction is conscious and in defiance of the Court.[14] Wasby has offered an alternative explanation. "[T]here are other instances," he states, "where one cannot easily attribute the impact to conscious resistance. It *may* be," he continues, "that the decisions have never reached the level at which they might be applied."[15]   The above findings substantiate Wasby's hypothesis. The ultimate targets of Supreme Court decisions are very often unaware of important decisions. They thus are often in unknowing, noncompliance with judicial mandates. Why this is so has been the major thrust of this text. The communication network through which the message must travel is clearly deficient in many respects. It is the purpose of the final chapter to offer some prescriptions to remedy this situation.

Notes

1. David Berlo, *The Process of Communication* (New York: Holt, Rinehart and Winston, 1960), p. 52.
2. Rochin v. California, 342 U. S. 165 (1952).
3. Miranda v. Arizona, 384 U. S. 436 (1966).
4. Harris v. New York, 401 U. S. 222 (1971).
5. Furman v. Georgia, 408 U. S. 238 (1972).
6. Florida, *Statutes Annotated,* sec. 775.082 (Supp. 1972).
7. The statute was ultimately held constitutional in *Proffitt* v. *Florida,* 44 U. S. L. W. 5229 (1976). It is clear that the rationale upon which *Furman* is based was ignored.
8. Walker v. Florida, 397 U. S. 387 (1970).
9. San Antonio v. Rodriguez, 411 U. S. 1 (1973).
10. See, e.g., Robert Birkby, "The Supreme Court and the Bible Belt: Tennessee Reaction to the 'Schempp' Decision," *Midwest Journal of Political Science,* 10 (August 1968), 304-15.
11. The breakdown is as follows: eighty-one public, twelve private religious, eight private nonsectarian, three unidentified.
12. Engel v. Vitale, 370 U. S. 421 (1962).
13. Dunn v. Blumstein, 405 U. S. 330 (1972).
14. See many of the studies in Theodore Becker and Malcolm Feeley (eds.), *The Impact of Supreme Court Decisions* (New York: Oxford University Press, 1973).
15. Stephen Wasby, "Police and the Law in Illinois: A First Look at the Communication of Supreme Court Decisions," *Public Affairs Bulletin,* 5 (September-October 1972), p. 1.

8 Recommendations and Prescriptions

As illustrated in Table 8-1 the publics themselves believe that the system of communicating Supreme Court decisions needs improvement. The foregoing analysis suggests that they are not wrong in their assessment. Indeed, glaring weaknesses in the system have been revealed throughout this study. Should the discussion end here, however, it would be no more than one-half completed. For the most crucial, but as yet unanswered, question has not been discussed: *What* can be done to improve the communication of Supreme Court decisions to the public?

Maintaining the Court's Legitimacy

The primary objective of the Court must be to maintain its high degree of legitimacy. This can be done in four main ways: (1) by recognizing its political nature and limited enforcement powers; (2) by avoiding the employment of political tactics utilized by the executive and legislative branches of government; (3) by avoiding scandal; and (4) by avoiding prolonged durations of tenure on the Court.

Limitations of the Court

In theory the Court is coequal with the other branches of government. Its edicts, again theoretically, are as binding as any legislative statute or executive order. However, the Court is fundamentally different from its counterparts. First, the method of selecting the Court's members prevents direct participation by the general populace. Appointment is for life. Only one justice, Samuel Chase, has been impeached, and he was not convicted. Additionally, only one justice (Fortas) has resigned under political pressure. Second, the rules guarding the Court's decisionmaking process are radically different from the other branches. Overt lobbying and direct political pressure of any type are uniformly improper in the judicial realm. Conversely, such tactics are widely accepted if not encouraged in the executive and legislative arenas. Third, and perhaps most important, the Court is drastically limited by its lack of enforcement power. It simply has no police force or army to insure

Table 8-1
Should the Communication of Supreme Court Decisions Be Improved?[a]

Occupational Group	Yes	No	Unsure
Doctors (N = 70)	34%	51%	14%
Attorneys (N = 84)	44	52	3
Judges (N = 112)	48	44	6
Clergy Members (N = 61)	65	24	10
School Teachers (N = 101)	64	22	12
Law Officers (N = 483)	80	12	5
Bookstore Operators (N = 29)	30	40	27
Moviehouse Operators (N = 15)	56	13	25
School Board Members (N = 26)	41	41	15
Lawmakers (N = 100)	53	34	8
Combined (N = 1081)	64	26	8

[a]Percentages do not total 100 percent because of a few "no responses."

compliance with its edicts. Finally, members of the judiciary operate under a different set of public expectations than do members of the other branches of government. This point will be elaborated on shortly.

The last two differences in particular demand that the Court act differently than its overtly political counterparts. It simply must not attempt to impose its collective will on American society. It must neither serve as an inflexible anchor to the nation, as was the case during the pre-Roosevelt Court days, nor outdistance contemporary thinking as was the case during the later Warren years.

Supporters of the present judicial system may shudder at the thought of what might have happened had Justices Roberts and Hughes not switched their votes when they did or what might have happened if the Warren Court had not come to an end with the death and retirement of several of its members. In the former case, the Court packing plan might have ultimately become successful, thereby destroying the stability accompanying a permanent nine-member body. Under the plan an additional member was to be appointed to the Court for each justice who did not voluntarily retire at age 70. The maximum number was set at 15. There are at least three negative effects of such a plan. First, the chances of a tie vote are increased, especially when the Court is comprised of an even number of justices. Second, the likelihood of greater infighting and a concomitant loss of congeniality generally found in small groups is increased. Finally, altering the size of the Court to accomplish political ends cannot but detract from the Court's credibility and prestige. Nonetheless, there was historical precedent for such action. Perhaps most well-known is Congress' reduction of the Court's membership from ten to eight during the presidency of Andrew Johnson, a political move to thwart the actions of an extremely unpopular president. Later, during the Grant administration, Congress restored one of those seats.

When the Warren Court greatly outdistanced American society in the late 1960s, equally appalling plans were suggested. Several constitutional amendments designed to override its edicts were offered in Congress. One of the most notable was the bill proposed by the late Senate Republican Minority Leader, Everett Dirksen. His proposal to overturn the *Reynolds* decision by allowing state senates to be apportioned on bases other than population fell only seven votes short of the necessary two-thirds majority required for passage in the U. S. Senate.[1] Similarly, numerous bills were submitted to Congress proposing amendments that would have overturned the school prayer and rights of defendants decisions.

Second, during the Warren Court era, several proposals to restrict the Court's appellate jurisdiction were advanced. Perhaps one of the most well known was a bill offered by Congressman William Tuck of Virginia. Opposed to the reapportionment decisions, he argued that jurisdiction over such matters be removed from the Court. He successfully guided legislation through the House of Representatives where it passed by a vote of 218 to 171. However, the bill died in the Senate.

Such action was based on an often cited precedent. In *Ex parte McCardle*[2] a Southern editor had been arrested for violating the Reconstruction Acts that were passed immediately after the Civil War. He petitioned for a writ of habeas corpus in the U. S. Circuit Court in Mississippi. Upon being denied, he appealed to the U. S. Supreme Court, which held unanimously that it had jurisdiction to hear the case. The arguments were presented, and the nation anxiously awaited the outcome. As Carl Swisher has stated, "It was widely believed that the Reconstruction Acts would be held unconstitutional."[3] The decision, however, was delayed despite the vehement protests of Justices Field and Grier. In the meantime, Congress passed a statute withdrawing

appellate jurisdiction in cases of McCardle's type. After repassage, because of
a veto by President Johnson, the Court heard argument about the constitution-
ality of Congress' action. Chief Justice Chase, writing for a unanimous Court,
noted that the power to regulate the Court's appellate jurisdiction had been
expressly granted to Congress (Article III). Thus, because Congress had with-
drawn jurisdiction over these types of appeals, the Court could not render
a judgment.

Third, during the Warren Court era a number of attempts were made to
impeach several of its members. Throughout the 1960s the John Birch Society
distributed bumper stickers calling for the impeachment of the Chief Justice.
Its accompanying campaign to accomplish this goal certainly detracted from
the prestige of the Court. Likewise, Representative Gerald Ford's attempt to
impeach Justice William O. Douglas cast suspicion on the Court's integrity.
Perhaps even more decidedly harmful was the controversy surrounding the
nomination of Associate Justice Fortas to the chief justiceship and his subsequent resignation from the Court. More of this matter will be discussed
shortly.

In sum, had the Warren Court era not terminated when it did, opponents
of the Court might have been successful in overturning or altering several of
its decisions, either by amendment, by restricting its jurisdiction, or by re-
moving some of its personnel. Any such action would certainly detract from
the Court's legitimacy.

How, then, may such occurrences be prevented? The answer lies in the
Court's ability to accurately assess the public's threshold of tolerance. The
primary means by which to do so is through utilization of the public opinion
poll. This readily available index may be employed by the Court to disclose
its relation to contemporary thinking. Some may perceive such a proposal as
reprehensible. After all, it has long been a fundamental doctrine in this
country that minority rights not be submitted to the majority vote. But let us
not be fooled. The Court has in its arsenal of weapons several devices that it
regularly employs when an issue is "too hot to handle." It has avoided many
confrontations by labeling cases moot, political, collusive, or unripe. It finds
that litigants lack standing and have not exhausted their lower court or administrative remedies. At other times when desiring to hear such cases the Court
simply becomes blind to these strategically invoked doctrines. What must be
remembered at all times is that the Court is a political institution that does
have a great deal of discretion. Once this is recognized, it is not as offensive
to suggest that the Court *more carefully* keep its eye on the public opinion
polls. None of this, of course, is intended to suggest that the Court avoid
producing creative constitutional law. Nor is this an argument on behalf of
judicial self-restraint, a concept which has philosophical as well as legal dimen-
sions. Rather the argument is a pragmatic one. Stated simply, the Court,
as with other political entities, has the latitude of "doing what it can get away

with." In part this can be determined by the Roper, Harris, and Gallup organizations.

Avoiding Political Tactics

Social science research clearly indicates that justices are expected to act in a manner different from congressmen and presidents. In his pioneering work entitled *Federal Courts in the Political Process,* Jack Peltason noted that judges are expected to withdraw from political activity, avoid direct criticism of public officials, not support controversial issues, appear indifferent to the outcome of interest group struggle, use temporate language, and avoid bias.[4] In short, a justice must place himself above pedestrian politics. If he does not, he violates the role expectations placed on him by society. In doing so he decreases the prestige enjoyed by the Court.

One of the most dearly held principles of the Court is that justices should not render advisory opinions. The concept is traceable to the Washington administration. Secretary of State Thomas Jefferson asked the Court for its opinion on a list of questions involving international law. The Court refused suggesting that it violated the separation of powers doctrine. Despite several instances of granting informal advice, to be noted shortly, the Court has fairly rigorously adhered to this precedent. To do otherwise today would be to violate what Wheeler has labeled "rigid expectations," actions that would certainly reduce the Court's legitimacy.[5]

Historically, a number of justices have participated in political activity. Many of the earliest justices were professional politicians before ascending the bench and continued such activity after appointment. For example, the Court's first chief justice, John Jay, twice ran for governor of New York while holding appointment. Further, he spent one year during that time on a diplomatic mission in England. Similarly, the Court's third chief justice, Oliver Ellsworth, was appointed by President Adams as Envoy to France while serving on the Court. Perhaps more extreme were the activities of Justices McLean (1829-1861) and Chase (1864-1873). While on the bench the former justice ran four times for the presidency. Chase had run twice before his appointment and again sought election while on the bench.

Past justices have not restricted their political activities to running for office. In one very famous instance of indiscretion, Justices Catron and Grier informed President Buchanan of the *Dred Scott*[6] decision in advance for political reasons. Perhaps equally appalling was the appointment of Justice Bradley to the Electoral Count Commission in the disputed presidential election of 1876. Indeed, he cast the deciding votes, which resulted in Rutherford B. Hayes being elected.

As the twentieth century dawned, however, such overt political activity became less and less acceptable. Constitutional amendments were introduced to prevent justices from seeking public office or from participating in campaigns. As Russell Wheeler has written:

> While justices have occasionally been mentioned for elective offices . . . there is by now a clear consensus that justices should avoid even passive connection with electoral campaigns, based on the fear that . . . the Court's *prestige* will be impaired by having its justices run for office.[7]

This is not to state that all political activity has ceased. Justice Jackson's aspirations for the presidency were well known. Justices continue to be asked to advise presidents. Recent examples include Frankfurther's and Byrne's relationship with Franklin D. Roosevelt, Vinson's relationship with Truman, and perhaps most scandalous, Fortas' relationship with Johnson. Indeed, it was Fortas' participation in important military and diplomatic conferences, his rendering of advice in racial policy matters, and his answering generally the President's calls for assistance that led to his forced resignation.[8]

Justices also continue to be asked to participate in various other governmental activities. Justice Jackson served as the U. S. Prosecutor at the Nuremberg Trials after World War II. Justice Vinson served as a secret negotiator with Russia, and President Kennedy asked Justice Goldberg to serve as a railroad labor arbitrator.[9]

Despite these incursions into the political arena, there have been relatively few such instances in recent U. S. history. This is particularly fortunate, for the public simply expects the Court to avoid such activity. When it does not, its members are attacked mercilessly as in the Fortas affair. This cannot but detract from the Court's prestige.

Avoiding Scandal

If the Court is to maintain its high degree of legitimacy, its members must, at all costs, avoid scandal. In matters of personal morality the public expects justices to be beyond reproach. One can only wonder what might have been the nation's reaction had Nominee Judge G. Harrold Carswell been appointed to the Court and subsequently charged with battery and attempting an "unnatural and lascivious act" after allegedly making homosexual advances toward a vice-squad officer.[10]

Another rigid expectation is that the justices not render decisions for financial reward or to secure personal gain. This has been a particularly acute problem in recent times, not only in the judiciary but in the legislative and executive branches as well. It is clear that the public will tolerate only so much from the overtly political arenas of government, let alone a branch

ostensibly removed from politics. One need look only to the dismissal of
presidential assistant Sherman Adams in 1958 for receiving certain "gifts" or to
the recent uproar over Congressman Sikes' improprieties to observe the public's
reaction to such activity. Even more demanding is the public's expectation
that justices not become involved in these and similar irregularities. The scan-
dals that erupted during the hearings surrounding Justice Fortas' nomination
to the chief justiceship are a case in point. His financial relationships with
foundations and individuals in past and possibly future litigation contributed
dramatically to his demise.[11] Subsequently the failure of Judge Clement
Haynesworth to be confirmed as his replacement is attributable, in part, to
his questionable involvement in the Vend-A-Matic Affair.[12] In that instance he
had purchased 1000 shares of stock at a cost of $16,230 before the case had
technically been completed.[13]

Another obvious situation, which must be carefully avoided, is in-court
fighting. Perhaps the most dastardly example of such activity is Justice
McReynold's treatment of Justices Brandeis and Cardozo. A blatant anti-
Semitic, he refused to speak to the former justice for the first three years of
his appointment, and during the swearing-in ceremony for the latter, he
conspicuously read a newspaper. He refused to sit next to Brandeis during the
Court's annual picture-taking session in 1924, and thus no picture was taken at
all. As Professor Abraham had written, "his personal demeanor on the bench
was a disgrace to the Court."[14]

Perhaps not as personally offensive to large segments of the public, but
assuredly as effective in diminishing the Court's prestige, was the well-publicized
feud between Justices Black and Jackson.[15]

Avoiding Prolonged Tenure

Justices of the Supreme Court have a reputation for their extreme longevity.
Indeed, they are not unfairly referred to as the nine, white-haired old men.
Many have served on the Court well into their seventies and some into their
eighties. In 1936, for example, the pre-Roosevelt Court was composed of
four justices who were in their sixties, four who were in their mid-seventies,
and Justice Brandeis who was eighty.

The temptation to remain on the Court for as long as possible historically has been a vexatious problem. Some justices have remained on the
Court far longer than propriety would dictate. For example, Justice McKinley
spent 15 years (1837-1852) on the Court, the greater part of which he was
absent due to illness. Similarly, Justice Field, in an attempt to break Justice
Marshall's length of tenure record, remained on the Court well past his
usefulness. Indeed, he was in extremely poor mental as well as physical
health when he was finally persuaded to resign. Recent justices have generally

not gone to this extreme. Indeed, it is to the lasting credit of Justices Whittaker, Frankfurter, Harlan, Black, and Warren that they stepped down when they did. Some have argued that Justice Douglas remained on the Court too long. Friends and enemies alike were disheartened by the sight of the crusty mountain climber and avid tennis player in his wheel chair being escorted from the hospital after his stroke. And his absence did require the rescheduling of several cases. Nevertheless, when it became clear to him that he could no longer perform his duties he immediately resigned.

Conclusion

In sum, if the Court is to retain its present structural characteristics, vast jurisdiction, and important role in the policymaking process, it must maintain its high esteem and elevated position in American society. Otherwise, it will find itself being attacked by the executive and legislative branches of government as well as by the general body politique. The extreme result might be a return of the Court to the pre-Marshall days, a Court lacking leadership and troubled by the problem of retaining competent personnel—indeed, a Court seriously lacking in authority and jurisdiction.

Facilitating the Media

One of the primary means by which to improve the communications process is to better facilitate the reporting of Supreme Court decisions. A number of suggestions have been offered in recent years, and several have been adopted. The Association of American Law Schools currently publishes a bulletin entitled *Preview*. The project was first suggested in 1963 by the Association's Committee on Education for Professional Responsibility. A Special Advisory Committee on Supreme Court decisions composed of distinguished law school professors throughout the United States was subsequently appointed to prepare short memoranda explaining the significance of Supreme Court cases, the issues involved, and possible alternative bases of decision.[16] The memoranda were reproduced and distributed through the Association's Washington office to the "regulars" who report the work of the Court for newspapers, wire services, radio, and television. A follow-up report was made juxtaposing the memoranda against the ultimate decision. Included were comments, corrections, and revisions. In 1964 cooperation was solicited from the news media and Chief Justice Earl Warren. The following year the committee prepared background memoranda on virtually all cases on the Court's oral argument docket.[17] By the end of the year there were 195 reporters on the mailing list. In 1966 the committee's report noted that press reaction had been enthusiastic and that cooperation from the law professors who prepared the memoranda had been excellent.[18] The project received continued support from the chief justice and the clerk of the court. By 1972 its funds were exhausted and no memoranda were written for the 1972-1973 term. The program was reinstated on a subscription basis in 1973.[19] About one-half of the cost is borne by the American Law Institute and the American Bar Association.[20] Currently, the service has 1643 subscribers (465 media subscribers), who receive about six issues per month containing two to four cases pending before the Court. Continuance of the program obviously is imperative.

Another reform that has been implemented, and which should be continued and improved on, is the practice initiated by Chief Justice Earl Warren of not delivering all decisions *en masse* on "Decision Monday."[21] However, as mentioned in Chapter 4 the reform has not always been followed.[22] Greater effort should be made in this respect, for it allows reporters more time to analyze and critique the most important cases. There will always be a problem during the month of June. The Court's most controversial cases are delivered at that time, generally because they are the toughest to decide and therefore require extensive deliberation. Nonetheless, the Court might issue the most newsworthy opinions on separate days. Indeed, the Burger Court is to be praised for not issuing its abortion, death penalty, and press "gag order" decisions all on one day at the end of the 1975-1976 term.

Another reform that has been implemented is the distribution of capsule summaries accompanying all written opinions. Judge Irving R. Kaufman, for one, had suggested the proposal.[23] Professor David Grey had asserted that this would be useful not only for the media, but also for hard-pressed legal scholars.[24] He had further argued that it would be beneficial for reporters to have such reports, even if the announcement of an opinion would be delayed a day or two.[25] Moreover, if strongly cautioned, reporters could quickly learn to treat summaries for exactly what they are, "helpful summary guidelines and *not* the decision of law handed down."[26]

Despite the aforementioned reforms, there are others that might be implemented to facilitate the media. In the first place, the services of the Public Information Office at the Supreme Court should be expanded. Reporters should be supplied with statistical and historical information about the justices, the Court itself, and the cases that come before it.[27] However, strong opposition is taken to the suggestion that the Office provide an "interpreter" of Supreme Court opinions.[28] The Court can ill afford to have a "Tenth Justice," indeed, a "Super-Justice," interpret its opinions. This is alien to historical and judicial thinking on the subject. Moreover, it often would heighten the confusion surrounding a decision. If interpreted incorrectly, a justice might feel compelled to offer clarifications and thus begin anew a long controversy and debate on the subject. Thus, the solution is not to supply "rewrites" of opinions, but rather to encourage, indeed demand, that justices write clearly and concisely so that reporters themselves can interpret the opinions.[29]   A more extensive analysis of this suggestion will be offered in the next section of this chapter.

A second means by which the media can be facilitated is the development of a "lockup" system.[30]   Often viewed as radical, the system would allow reporters to be placed in a room having no outside access.   There, they would be given copies of decisions that the Court is about to render.   In this manner the reporters would have a number of hours in which to digest the opinions and thus report them with a greater degree of accuracy.   After the Court had officially and publicly announced its decision, reporters would be released and allowed to call their stories in to their editors.   This practice would in no way compromise the historical practice and necessity of maintaining strict secrecy about the Court's decisions until they have been formally rendered.   Such a proposal was made to Chief Justice Burger in 1969 by regular members of the Supreme Court press corps.   He responded by stating that he believed the reform was too advanced for its time.[31]   Perhaps he might now wish to reconsider his thinking.[32]

Improving the Message

In 1959 the distinguished professor Henry M. Hart, Jr. wrote, "The Court would better serve its function . . . if it tried to decide fewer cases and to write in those fewer cases better-reasoned opinions."[33]   In expressing this sentiment he is reflecting the general consensus of the scholarly community toward judicial opinions.   For decades observers of the Court have been critical, not only of the excessive numbers of opinions, but most importantly, of the style in which they have been written.

Number and Length of Opinions

Ever since Warren Burger assumed the chief justiceship he has taken the lead in urging reform of the judiciary.   He blames the archaic state of the system on the fact that the legal profession did not heed Roscoe Pound's early warnings to bring methods, machinery, and personnel up to date.[34]   He has also noted that problems have become far more serious than anticipated because of the dramatic increase in population: from 67 million in 1900 to 205 million in 1970.   Compounding the problems created by this trend is the fact that entirely new types of cases have been added to court dockets.   As a result, the Supreme Court's workload had increased tremendously.   For example, during Chief Justice Stone's tenure (1941-1946) the number of cases docketed increased by 158 (from 1302 to 1460).   In marked contrast, during the five years between 1967-1971, docketed cases increased by 956 (from 3559 to 4515).[35]

Obviously the Court is under tremendous pressure. Its membership has remained stable at nine since 1869, and few would seriously suggest that the number be expanded to accommodate the increase in workload. Rather, other remedies have been proposed. The chief justice himself is a strong proponent of eliminating three-judge district courts and all direct appeals to the Supreme Court.[36] The Freund Committee, a distinguished group of legal scholars appointed under the aegis of the Federal Judicial Center, has proposed that a National Court of Appeals be created, which would screen the mass of petitions for review. As the report states:

Petitions for review would be filed initially in the National Court of Appeals. The great majority, it is to be expected, would be finally denied by that court. Several hundred would be certified annually to the Supreme Court for further screening and choice of cases to be heard and adjudicated there. Petitions found to establish a true conflict between the circuits would be granted by the National Court of Appeals and the cases heard and finally disposed of there, except as to those petitions deemed important enough for certification to the Supreme Court.[37]

In similar fashion the Congressional Commission on the Revision of the Federal Court Appellate System, chaired by Senator Roman L. Hruska, has recommended a national court of appeals to help eliminate some of the workload of the Supreme Court. Unlike the Freund court, it would not screen petitions initially. Rather, it would hear cases referred to it by the Supreme Court or transferred to it by one of the courts of appeal.[38] Several other proposals have been advanced as well.[39] Although the chief justice has not outrightly endorsed the concept of a new court, he has implicitly done so by stating that "if other remedial measures are not adopted, the creation of such a court is inevitable."[40]

The aforementioned proposals have one element in common. They emphasize external reforms to help alleviate the tremendous burden under which the Court currently operates. Indeed, most suggestions have been in this vein. There have also, however, been some steps taken toward reforming the system from within. For example Chief Justice Burger has catalogued the following: admission to the Supreme Court bar by written motion rather than formal ceremony,[41] elimination of the lengthy announcement of opinions in favor of brief statements, and reduction of oral argument from one to one-half hour for each side (1970).[42]

A number of additional internal reforms have been suggested by the Freund Committee. Among them are: changing the "Rule of Four" in granting certiorari petitions to a rule of five or six (the committee ultimately opposed this reform); not setting cases for reargument simply to conform to the principle that all cases finally argued during that term are decided at that term; eliminating oral argument in some cases; utilizing older and more experienced clerks for greater periods of time;[43] and providing more secretarial aid to clerks and justices alike.[44]   However, one can readily observe that none of these reforms or proposals has required the justices themselves to take any position action. Indeed, they are very passive reforms, requiring little if any effort on their part.

What has been overlooked by nearly all the reform groups and reformers is that the Court itself can do much to improve its efficiency and thereby reduce the extremely heavy workload. In the process the quality of the Court's messages will be improved. First, incumbent justices should refrain from writing excessive numbers of concurring and dissenting opinions, a practice that has radically increased during the past few decades. Opinions written because of minor variations with the majority or minority can and should be eliminated. They serve few functions, are generally ignored by the scholarly community, and often add confusion to the issues at hand. Second, the justices should work diligently to reduce the length of their opinions. As Judge Herbert Gregory long ago pointed out, the purpose of an opinion is to decide a case, "not to expound legal philosophy" or to write "an ideal piece of legal literature. Nor," he continues, "is it necessary to exhaust all the law and cite all the cases."[45] It was his thesis that not only were too many opinions handed down, but that a great number of cases were "unnecessarily long."[46] Often such opinions, he claimed, contained too much dicta. Likewise, D. W. Stevenson writing in 1975 noted that it was a habit of writers "to put far more than they need" into an opinion.[47]

Table 6-1 illustrated that the average length of majority opinions increased from 9.1 and 8.0 pages in 1949 and 1954, respectively, to 16.4 in 1974. With the tremendous increase in workload (the Court wrote only 87 majority opinions in 1949 as compared to 122 in 1974), the quality of the opinion (message) cannot help but decline. Likewise, the length of concurring and dissenting opinions has increased, again adding to the workload of the justices. It is suggested that in these opinions a comprehensive restatement of the facts is unnecessary. Nor is it necessary to reiterate points of agreement.

Thus, justices should make strong efforts to contain their enthusiasm for preciseness. Where they feel compelled, a brief statement will be sufficient to express their differences with the majority or the dissent. This not only will facilitate reducing the workload of the Court, but also will improve the quality of the message. It is with this topic that we now turn.

Quality of the Opinion

John P. Frank clearly has written the most extended and scathing critique of Supreme Court messages.[48] Although his work was first published in 1958, its message is as relevant today as it was then. Indeed, it appears that most of the justices since that time have paid scant attention to his suggestions. Without exception, every justice has, at times, been less than clear, has failed to write for the educated public, and has written in a convoluted style utilizing unnecessary legalisms, excessive footnoting, and archaic prose. Indeed, this has been the rule rather than the exception.

Of paramount importance is that the justices keep in mind whom they are writing for. As Stevenson has written, "Too often . . . judges write as if only the writer counted. Too often they write as if to themselves . . . ."[49] We are no longer living in the eighteenth century when the masses were relatively uneducated. No longer is a majority of the nation illiterate. Conversely, vast numbers of the general populace are highly educated. Many individuals have an intense interest in the work of the Supreme Court, among them school teachers, members of minority groups, and members of occupational groups that must deal with Court rulings on a regular, if not day-to-day, basis. Moreover, a large number of other individuals have an occasional interest in what the Court has to say. Thus, the Court no longer is observed exclusively by the legal community. It is as important for the police officer as it is for the attorney to be cognizant of many of its opinions. Indeed, it may be even more important in many instances, such as with the case of *Miranda* and similar defendant's rights decisions. As Stevenson has written, judges "must realize that the purpose of an opinion is to make a judgment credible to a diverse audience of readers."[50]

With the realization that it is writing for a much broader audience than originally envisioned, the Court will no doubt feel compelled to alter drastically its archaic writing practices. Not only will the general public welcome the change, but many members of the legal community, including a number of leading lawyers and judges, will be most thankful as well. As has been noted, "There is nothing requiring that Supreme Court opinions be less than lucid."[51] The question becomes, how can this be accomplished. The answer is multifold.

First, justices should be made aware of the fact that generally they are poor writers. This can be brought to their attention by serious, sustained, disinterested, and competent criticism of their opinions in the law reviews and bar journals.[52]

Second, justices should shorten the time lapse between the decisionmaking conferences and the drafting of their opinions.[53] In this manner the briefs need not be reread, the facts reassembled, or the authorities resurveyed. As a result, unnecessary duplication of effort is avoided.

Third, justices should establish the practice of critiquing and rewriting their own opinions. Helpful in this endeavor are leading books on writing style. Judge George Rose Smith of the Arkansas Supreme Court, who has written an invaluable tract on this subject, suggests that William Strunk's volume entitled, *The Elements of Style,* H. W. Fowler's *Modern English Usage,* Theodore Bernstein's *The Careful Writer,* and Bergen's and Evans' *Contemporary American Usage* were especially useful to him.[54] Moreover, the justices should be made aware of the few articles that do exist on opinion writing.[55]

Fourth, the justices should carefully avoid the use of legalisms. Judge Smith has defined a legalism thusly: "A word or phrase that a lawyer might use in drafting a contract or a pleading but would not use in conversation with his wife."[56] He offers five examples: *said* in the sense of *aforesaid; same* and *such* in a similar sense; *hereafter called,* and *inter alia.* Many would agree with Judge Smith's conclusion about the use of these and other phrases. "I absolutely and unconditionally guarantee," he states, "that the use of legalisms in your opinions will destroy whatever freshness and spontaneity you might otherwise attain."[57]

A fifth manner in which the style of opinions may be improved involves the use of footnotes. Excessive use of footnotes is now common in most opinions. One often has the impression that they are inserted simply to impress the reader. Obviously this should be avoided.

There is some debate over the type of style that should be utilized in footnoting. John Frank writes approvingly of the recent change whereby citations are now placed at the bottom of the page.[58] He claims that this makes the text easier to read. And indeed it does. One need only look at his example of Justice Stone's dissent in *Rabnic* v. *McBride* to recognize this.[59] On the other hand Judge Smith has suggested that this practice requires "the reader to interrupt his chain of thought by dropping his eyes to the bottom of the page."[60] Perhaps a compromise of the two approaches is best. Once a citation has been made to a reference, subsequent notation is unnecessary. Brief citations, it is suggested, might be better placed in the text where the reader may simply skim over them.[61] Footnoting should be reserved for those citations that are long and contain additional substantive information.

Finally, it is proposed that the chief justices appoint a special committee on style to conduct an in-depth study into the best methods of opinion writing. The body itself should be composed of distinguished judges and lawyers, as well as professors of English, history, political science, and law. The committee should consider, among other things, recommending a general outline that should be followed in opinion writing. It should make recommendations on the usage of Latin phrases and legalisms. These proposals might then be adopted by the Court as binding on its members. This would promote uniformity in style and hopefully improve the quality of the message. If nothing else, the existence of the committee would serve to heighten the consciousness among Supreme Court justices that there is a need to improve their opinion writing.

Strengthening the Channels

In Chapter 5 it was observed that there are two groups of publics that receive Supreme Court messages: continuous publics (attorneys, judges, law enforcement officers, and lawmakers), and intermittent publics (doctors, clergy members, school teachers, bookstore operators, moviehouse operators, and school board members). Continuous publics, those having the greatest need for accurate information, utilize the most reliable channels: specialized memoranda, bulletins, and newsletters, specialized magazines or journals, and the opinions themselves. On the other hand, intermittent publics rely heavily on radio, television, and general periodicals. There is little doubt that each of the channels of communication relied on by both publics needs to be drastically improved if Supreme Court messages are to be accurately transmitted to the decoders and receivers.

Electronic Media

It is fortunate that the continuous publics do not rely on radio and television as channels of information. Although these media have such advantages as delivering news first, without cost (once the television or radio is owned), while an individual is doing other things, and requiring a minimal amount of mental effort,[62] they are clearly not the best means of communicating Supreme Court messages. These media are simply not able to devote enough time to a story to be of extended value.[63]

Some have advocated that the Court reconsider its position and allow live broadcasts and telecasts to be transmitted from the courtroom.[64] This practice might elevate the general level of cognizance about the Court and its procedures. However, opinions are only briefly summarized when delivered. Thus, live coverage would be of little value in improving the communication of Supreme Court *decisions* to the public.

To improve the communication of Supreme Court decisions, radio and television must upgrade the quality of the stories they transmit. This can only be done by improving the quality of those reporting and writing them. Presently no network assigns a full-time correspondent to the Court. Furthermore, it is unlikely that any will do so in the near future, due to the expense involved. Thus, heavy reliance has been, and will continue to be, placed on the wire services for such information. Therefore it is imperative that the personnel employed by these agencies be highly trained, experienced, and well-versed in the concomitants of judicial decisionmaking. The wire services can also improve their coverage of the Court by more spot analyses of issues and cases and by carrying monthly or weekly columns on legal news and issues.[65]

Despite the above suggestions, it is doubtful that radio and television will ever become useful sources of information about Supreme Court decisions. They simply have too many inherent limitations. Furthermore, they are rarely *preferred* as a channel from which to obtain such information when compared to the written media (see Table 8-2). Moreover, no group of respondents to the survey selected electronic media as their *best* channel of information (see Table 8-3).

Table 8-2
Preferred Channels from Which to Obtain Information about
Supreme Court Decisions[a]

Channel	First Choice	Second Choice	Third Choice	Fourth Choice
Written Materials (N = 1047)	72%	14%	6%	3%
Electronic Media (N = 1012)	12	38	27	14
Lecturer or Speaker (N = 1014)	16	31	31	13
Informal Conversation (N = 1002)	5	13	18	54

[a]Percentages do not total 100 percent because of a few "no responses."

Table 8-3
Best Channel of Information about Supreme Court Decisions

Written Materials Newspapers, Reports, Magazines	Electronic Media Radio and Television	Lecturer or Speaker	Informal Conversation
70.4% (N = 1130)	5.0% (N = 82)	12.9% (N = 207)	11.5% (N = 185)

Written Materials

Newspapers clearly have several advantages over the electronic media in communicating Supreme Court messages to target publics. Not only does this medium allow the recipient to proceed at his own pace at a convenient time, it most importantly has the advantage of being able to deliver more detailed and extensive coverage than either radio or television. Nonetheless, it is this channel, the channel that has the greatest potential of reaching the largest numbers of people, that has failed most miserably to date. How frustrating it is for the Court enthusiast to run to the newsstand to read about the Court's latest decision on the death penalty, abortion, and newsmen's gag orders, only to come away with far more questions than answers. Stories are disjointed, misleading, and often almost totally lacking in substantive information about the decision. As with radio and television, great reliance is placed on the wire service for information. Thus, improvement must take place there. However, much more can be done. The reporters who are assigned to cover the work of the Court should be experienced and trained specifically in the workings of the judicial system. Furthermore, they should not be rotated out of the position once they have gained the knowledge that would enable them to report on the Court with some skill.

Newspaper editors can also do much to improve the smooth flow of decisions. First, they can encourage the publication of more articles relating to the Court. Second, they should watch carefully the multiple editing of articles that generally takes place. This often results in great distortions. Third, they should make sure that the headline is accurate, rather than just a catchy phrase to sell papers. Finally, as one astute observer of the press has suggested, they "might well subordinate the practice of breakneck competition enough to insure real precision of reporting."[66]

Unfortunately, as with radio and television, the suggested reforms are likely to fall on deaf ears. After all, many of these proposals are well-known and have been advocated for quite some time.[67] The constraints of time and money as well as the general lack of commitment on the part of the press make for a pessimistic outlook. Fortunately, those who most need to receive accurate information about the Court (judges, attorneys, and law enforcement officers) rely the least on this channel.

Periodicals, both general and specialized, offer the greatest potential of accurately transmitting Supreme Court decisions to the public. In part this is because of the nature of the media. They have all the advantages of newspapers without many of the latter's disadvantages. Periodicals can provide detailed coverage of decisions. At the same time they are not subject to the hasty reporting and editorializing characteristics of newspapers. The authors of articles have a few days to digest the decisions, compile background material, and develop insightful analysis. The major problem, as was noted in Chapter 5, is that magazines and periodicals often do not carry articles on the Court. Thus, editors must be strongly encouraged to give more extended coverage of its decisions. This is particularly true of the specialized journals. How this should be undertaken will be discussed shortly.

It might be suggested that specialized memoranda on specific Supreme Court decisions be mailed by that body to the various target publics that it affects. Obviously, this would be far too expensive to be practical. On the other hand, private groups might be encouraged to pass along information via this method. For example the American Bar Association, the American Medical Association, and various organizations representing other target groups might send summaries of decisions to its official membership. This channel, of course, is most useful in organizations that are organized in a highly bureaucratic manner. These groups, especially law enforcement agencies, employ regularized lines of communication. As such it is rather easy for them to utilize interoffice communiques to pass along information about Supreme Court decisions.

Lecturers or Speakers

Tables 8-2 and 8-3 illustrate that not only is the lecturer or speaker preferred as
a channel from which to obtain information about the Supreme Court by many
of the respondents, but it is perceived as the best channel by many as well. Indeed, in both respects this method was chosen ahead of the electronic media and
informal conversation. However, it should be noted that the figures are skewed
because of the large number of law enforcement officers in the sample. Overwhelmingly they chose this means as a best channel of information (22 percent,
$N = 154$). In fact no more than 5 percent of any other group chose this channel. The reason for this should be readily apparent. Law enforcement officers
are required by state law to enroll in classes for instruction about their job.
They must regularly attend refresher courses.[68] The fact that the one group that
does come into regular contact with lecturers and speakers rates them very
highly is suggestive of a prescription for improving the accuracy and efficacy of
communicating Supreme Court decisions to target publics.

Final Prescription

It was argued earlier that the Supreme Court Public Information Officer (Press
Officer) should not become the interpreter of Supreme Court decisions.[69] It was
advanced that he should neither interpret nor offer conjecture about opinions
for the media. This should not be taken to mean, however, that he and his
office can do nothing to facilitate the smooth flow of decisions to target publics.
Indeed, it is the office that should be charged with this responsibility. The
Public Information Officer, more than any other official, occupies a position
critical to the improvement of the communications process. He has ready access
to Court opinions and to the Supreme Court library. Moreover, he already services the news media to some extent and thus is familiar with many of their
needs.

It is proposed that the duties of the Public Information Officer be expanded
to include:

1. Supplying occupationally relevant periodicals with information about
   Supreme Court decisions that are pertinent to their readership.
2. Making available to general news magazines the same information as above.
3. Encouraging governmental agencies to develop seminars and programs to
   explain Supreme Court decisions relevant to their fields of endeavor.
4. Encouraging private associations, foundations, and agencies to do the same
   as above.
5. Encouraging private associations, foundations, and agencies to distribute
   to their membership information about relevant Supreme Court decisions.

6. Encouraging academic institutions, such as junior colleges, colleges, and universities, to offer courses on the Court's decisions.
7. Encouraging vocational and technical institutions to offer courses on the Court's decisions.
8. Sponsoring seminars for high school social studies teachers to enable them to become familiar with the Court's policies.
9. Sponsoring graduate seminars for college professors in the social sciences to enable them to become familiar with the Court's policies.

The Office should maintain a complete list of periodicals, journals, and bulletins disseminated by the various occupational groups. When the Court renders an opinion, the office should immediately mail a copy of it along with supporting information to the editor of the appropriate publication. Telephone contact should be made with editors when possible to encourage cooperation in covering the work of the Supreme Court. Further, the information should be made available to magazines of general circulation on request.

The Office should also encourage governmental agencies to disseminate information about Supreme Court decisions via special training sessions, conferences, workshops, and refresher courses. There is some precedent for this idea and strong evidence that it is a useful and well-received means of conveying decisions. Immediately after the *Miranda* decision the Federal Bureau of Investigation established training centers to explain the decision.[70] In a survey of small-town Wisconsin police officers who attended some of them, it was found that these meetings were identified most often as the first and best source of information about *Miranda*.[71] Furthermore, of all the decisions inquired of, it was the only one about which the officers retained a high level of substantive knowledge. The seminars, because they were sponsored by the FBI, lent a degree of prestige to the setting. Officers were proud to state that they had attended, and they rated the seminars as invaluable. This study reinforces the earlier finding by Neal Milner that policemen in four large cities in Wisconsin considered training and conference sessions to be most effective.[72]

The Office should encourage private associations, foundations, and agencies to inform their groups about relevant Supreme Court opinions. This can be accomplished in several ways. First, contact should be made with the regular governing boards of these associations publicizing the services offered by the Office. Small grants might be made to professional groups to aid them in developing seminars and lectures on important decisions. They should also be encouraged to include information about decisions in their newsletters, memoranda, and bulletins.

Encouragement should also be extended to teachers and institutions of higher learning. This, too, can be undertaken in several ways. First, materials disseminated by the Office should be made available to social studies and social science teachers at both the high school and university levels. This will allow them to remain thoroughly informed about the Court. Vocational schools can be encouraged to participate by a series of small grants to pay instructors to teach specific courses on the Court and its decisions. At major universities where large continuing education departments are often found, similar funding could take place. Finally seminars could be developed throughout the United States to train teachers at all levels of instruction about the importance and substantive thrust of Supreme Court decisions.

In the seminars, conferences, or training sessions mentioned above, the Office should provide only copies of the actual opinions with supporting background information and data (and possibly a limited amount of funding). It should *not* provide interpretive information. This should be left to the individual seminar director, who is hired by the occupational group cosponsoring the lecture. This should be made clear to each audience. In this fashion the Office is able to maintain a neutral posture toward Court opinions. Thus, it does not run the risk of misinterpreting the policy of the Supreme Court or of acting as a tenth justice.

Conclusions

Prior to the past three decades, the Supreme Court's policymaking role was very much underrated, if not ignored. With the rise of behavioralism after World War II and the employment of improved techniques with which to evaluate the judicial process, this misperception was exploded, at least among academics. Nonetheless, a large segment of the American public still remains uninformed about the Court and its policies. It has been the underlying assumption of this study that such a situation should not exist, especially in a democratic society where the citizenry is expected to rationally and directly choose many of its leaders by utilizing the franchise. To remedy the situation actors involved in each ingredient of the communications process must endeavor to improve the strength of their link. The justices themselves, it has been suggested, can do much to aid in the improvement of the system. Wireservice, newspaper, magazine, and television reporters and their editors likewise carry a great share of the burden. Other decoders, especially the leaders of occupational groups, can do much to improve the clarity and reliability with which Supreme Court messages are disseminated. Institutions of higher learning can do much to train lawyers, journalists, teachers, and even the justices themselves. It is incumbent on all these individuals to do their utmost to establish the smooth flow of policy decisions to target publics. Otherwise compliance with Supreme Court decisions may be merely accidental. Similarly, noncompliance simply may be the result of ignorance on the part of the electorate.

Notes

1. Reynolds v. Sims, 377 U. S. 533 (1964).

2. Ex parte McCardle, 7 Wall. 506 (1869).

3. Carl Swisher, *American Constitutional Development* (Cambridge, Mass.: The Riverside Press, 1954), p. 324.

4. Jack Peltason, *Federal Courts in the Political Process* (New York: Random House, 1955), p. 21.

5. Russell Wheeler, "Extra Judicial Behavior and the Role of Supreme Court Justices," *University Programs Modular Studies* (Morristown, N. J.: General Learning Press, 1975), p. 12.

6. Dred Scott v. Sanford, 19 How. 393 (1857).

7. Wheeler, *supra* note 5 (emphasis added).

8. Henry Abraham, *Justices and Presidents* (New York: Oxford University Press, 1974), p. 263. For a thorough account of the Fortas affair see Robert Shogan, *A Question of Judgment* (Indianapolis: Bobbs-Merrill Co., 1972).

9. For other examples see John Frank, *Marble Palace: The Supreme Court in American Life* (New York: Alfred A. Knopf, 1968), pp. 268-69.

10. See *Gainesville Sun,* July 11, 1976, p. 18; and July 19, 1976, p. 5A.

11. See Joel Grossman and Stephen Wasby, "Haynesworth and Parker: History Does Live Again," *South Carolina Law Review,* 23 (1971), 353.

12. For an extended analysis see John Steele, "Haynesworth v. the U. S. Senate (1969)," *Fortune*, 81 (March 1970), 90-95.

13. Ibid.

14. Abraham, *supra* note 8, p. 166.

15. For a thorough analysis see Eugene Gerhart, *America's Advocate: Robert H. Jackson* (New York: Bobbs-Merrill Co., 1958), Chapter 15; and Charlotte Williams, *Hugo L. Black: A Study in the Judicial Process* (Baltimore: Johns Hopkins Press, 1950), pp. 177-86.

16. Report of the Special Advisory Committee on Supreme Court Decisions (Washington, D. C.: Association of American Law Schools, 1964), Part 1, p. 164.

17. A Report of the Special Committee on Supreme Court Decisions (Washington, D.C.: Association of American Law Schools, 1966), Part 1, p. 324.

18. For comments see ibid., pp. 326-27.

19. Everette Dennis, "Another Look at Press Coverage of the Supreme Court," *Villanova Law Review,* 20 (March 1975), 788.

20. *Gainesville Sun,* December 10, 1975, p. 8A.

21. John MacKenzie, "The Warren Court and the Press," *Michigan Law Review,* 67 (December 1968), 305, n. 8. Another often mentioned aid to reporters has been the change of starting time for its meetings from noon to 10:00 A.M.

22. Mark Cannon, Administrative Assistant to the Chief Justice, has

concluded that in recent times about half of the opinions have been delivered on days other than the first court day in the week. See Mark Cannon, "An Administrator's View of the Supreme Court," *Federal Bar News,* 22 (April 1975), 112-13.

23. Irving Kaufman, "The Courts and the Public: A Problem in Communication," *American Bar Association Journal,* 54 (December 1968), 1193.

24. David Grey, *The Supreme Court and the News Media* (Evanston, Ill.: Northwestern University Press, 1968), p. 143.

25. Ibid.

26. Ibid.

27. During his confirmation hearings, Nominee Fortas suggested that reporters should be provided with such information. See MacKenzie, *supra* note 21, at 315.

28. See, e.g., Grey, *supra* note 24, p. 142; and Lionel Sobel, "News Coverage of the Supreme Court," *American Bar Association Journal,* 56 (June 1970), 550.

29. See Chapter 4.

30. See, e.g., Grey, *supra* note 24, p. 144.

31. Seth Goldschlager, "The Law and the Mass Media," (Unpublished thesis, Yale Law School, 1971), p. 275.

32. See MacKenzie, *supra* note 21, at 315.

33. Henry Hart, "The Supreme Court 1958 Term, Forward: The Time Chart of the Justices," *Harvard Law Review,* 73 (November 1959), 101.

34. Warren Burger, "The State of the Federal Judiciary," in Howard James (ed.), *Crisis in the Courts* (New York: David McKay Co., 1971), p. v.

35. *Report of the Study Group on the Caseload of the Supreme Court* (Washington, D. C.: Federal Judicial Center, 1972), p. iv.

36. See Commission on Revision of the Federal Court Appellate System, *Structure and Internal Procedures: Recommendations for Change* (Washington, D. C.: 1975), p. 176.

37. *Report of the Study Group on the Caseload of the Supreme Court, supra* note 35, p. 18.

38. Commission on Revision of the Federal Court Appellate System, *supra* note 36, pp. 30-39.

39. See, e.g., William Alsup, "A Policy Assessment of the National Court of Appeals," *Hastings Law Journal,* 25 (May 1974), 1313-49; Elberhard Deutsch, "The National Court of Appeals," *Judicature,* 59 (November 1974), 180-83; Paul Freund, "A National Court of Appeals," *Hastings Law Journal,* 25 (May 1974), 1301-12; Clement Haynesworth, "A New Court to Improve the Administration of Justice," *American Bar Association Journal,* 59 (August 1973), 841-45; and Maurice Rosenberg, "Planned Flexibility to Meet Changing Needs of the Federal Appellate System," *Cornell Law Review,* 59 (April 1974), 576-96.

40. Commission on the Revision of the Federal Court Appellate System, *supra* note 36, p. 178.

41. This practice was established in 1971. Presently about 80 percent of the 5000 yearly applicants are admitted in this manner.

42. Commission on the Revision of the Federal Court Appellate System, *supra* note 36, p. 174.

43. Presently each justice has three clerks. They are generally chosen from the top rank of their law school class and serve for one or two terms.

44. *Report of the Study Group on the Caseload of the Supreme Court, supra* note 35, pp. 39-46.

45. Herbert Gregory, "Shorter Judicial Opinions," *Virginia Law Review,* 34 (1948), 364. In this instance he was specifically referring to Virginia Supreme Court messages.

46. Ibid., at 362.

47. D W Stevenson, "Writing Effective Opinions," *Judicature,* 59 (October 1975), 134, 135.

48. Frank, *supra* note 9.

49. Stevenson, *supra* note 47, at 134.

50. Ibid.

51. "On Covering the Court," *Columbia Journalism Review,* 1 (Fall 1962), 2.

52. See Hart, *supra* note 33, at 125.

53. See George Smith, "A Primer of Opinion Writing for Four New Judges," *Arkansas Law Review,* 21 (Summer 1967), 197-212.

54. Ibid., at 207-08.

55. See, e.g., those cited herein.

56. Smith, *supra* note 53, at 209.

57. Ibid.

58. Frank, *supra* note 9, p. 131.

59. Ibid., pp. 297-98.

60. Smith, *supra* note 53, at 211.

61. For example, the footnote stating *italics supplied* could be regularly handled in this manner. See Smith, *supra* note 53, at 212.

62. William Stephenson, *The Play Theory of Mass Communication* (Chicago: University of Chicago Press, 1967), pp. 22-23.

63. These media do serve the function of alerting decoders and receivers to the fact that opinions have been rendered.

64. See MacKenzie, *supra* note 21, at 315.

65. Dennis, *supra* note 19, at 784.

66. "On Covering the Court," *supra* note 51. See also MacKenzie, *supra* note 21, at 303.

67. See Grey, *supra* note 24.

68. See Stephen Wasby, "Police Training and Criminal Procedure," *The*

Police Chief, 139 (October 1972), 24-31; and Stephen Wasby, "Police and the Law in Illinois: A First Look at the Communication of Supreme Court Decisions," *Public Affairs Bulletin,* 5 (September-October 1972), pp. 6-8.

69. For an historical discussion of this office see Dennis, *supra* note 19, at 778. See also Grey, *supra* note 24, pp. 46-48.

70. See Stephen Wasby, "The Communication of the Supreme Court's Criminal Procedure Decisions: A Preliminary Mapping," *Villanova Law Review,* 18 (June 1973), 1097-98.

71. Larry Berkson, "The United States Supreme Court and Small Town Police Officers: A Study in Communication," (Unpublished manuscript, 1970).

72. Neal Milner, *The Court and Local Law Enforcement: The Impact of Miranda* (Beverly Hills, Cal.: Sage Publications, 1971), pp. 94-95.

**Appendix A
Survey Return Rates**

Public	Universe	Sample	Number Returned	Return Rate
Bookstore Operators	unknown	100	30	30%
Clergy Members	unknown	186	62	33%
County Commissioners	355	91	11	12%
Doctors	unknown	200	70	35%
Judges, Circuit	261	261	75	29%
Judges, County	154	154	40	26%
Mayors	118	118	34	29%
Moviehouse Operators	unknown	100	16	16%
Police Chiefs	157	157	57	36%
Policemen	unknown	270	143	53%
Private Attorneys	12,852	48	16	33%
Public Defenders	20	20	13	65%
Public Defenders' Assistants	269	55	14	25%
Representatives	120	120	45	38%
School Board Members	347	87	27	31%
School Teachers	unknown	200	104	52%
Senators	40	40	16	40%
Sheriffs	67	67	29	43%
Sheriffs' Deputies	unknown	237	96	40%
State Troopers	1026	425	172	40%
State Attorneys	20	20	16	80%
State Attorneys' Assistants	408	52	25	48%

**Appendix B
Specialized Literature Listed
as Channels of Information
about Supreme Court
Decisions**

Public	Literature[a]
Doctors	*Journal of the American Medical Association, Journal of the Florida Medical Association, Journal of Legal Medicine, The Journal of Psychiatry, Medical Economics, Medical World News, New England Journal of Medicine, Pediatrics*
Attorneys	*American Bar Association Journal, American Criminal Law Quarterly, American Trial Lawyers Association Journal, Anti-Trust Trade Regulation Report, The Barrister, Case and Comment, Civil Liberties, Criminal Law Bulletin, Criminal Law Reporter, Florida Bar Journal, Georgetown Law Journal, Harvard Law Review, Judicature, Legal Aid Briefcase, Opinions of the Attorney General of Florida, The Prosecutor, Search and Seizure Bulletin, Securities Law Review, Trial, University of Chicago Review of Court Terms*
Judges	*American Bar Association Journal, American Law Quarterly, Barrons, Case and Comment, Civil Liberties, Criminal Law Bulletin, Decision, Florida Bar Journal, Harvard Law Review, Judicature, Juvenile Court Judges Journal, Opinions of the Attorney General of Florida, Oyez Oyez, Search and Seizure Bulletin, Southwestern Law Journal, Stetson Intramural Law Review, Texas Bar Journal, Trial*
Clergy Members	*The Christian Century, Christianity and Crisis, Christianity Today, Commentary, Dateline, The Gospel Advocate, Journal of Religion, Presbyterian Survey, Social Action, United Methodists Today*
School Teachers	*American Scholar, Childhood Education, Education Digest, Educational Forum, Florida Education Association Tabloid, Florida Schools, National Association of Secondary School Principals Bulletin, Phi Delta Kappan, Today's Education*
Bookstore Operator	*The Center Magazine, Publisher's Weekly*
Law Enforcement Officers	*American Legion Magazine, County News, Crime Control Digest, Criminal Justice Newsletter, Criminal Law Bulletin, Criminal Law Reporter, Criminology and Police Science, Drug Enforcement, FBI Law Enforcement Bulletin, Florida on Patrol, Florida Police, Florida Police Chief, The Florida Sheriff, Florida Sheriff's Star, Identification News, Journal of Criminal Law, Juris Doctor, Law and Order, Opinion of the Attorney General of Florida, Police Chief, Police Research Bulletin, REAA Newsletter, Search and Seizure Bulletin, State Peace Officers Journal, Traffic Safety, Trial*
Moviehouse Operators	*Box Office, Independent Film Journal, N.A.T.O of Florida*
School Board Members	*The American School Board Journal, American Schools and Universities, Florida PTA Bulletin, Florida Schools, Nation's Schools, Phi Delta Kappan*
Lawmakers	*American Bar Association Journal, American City, American Jewish Historical Quarterly, Civil Liberties, Council of State Governments Bulletin, Criminal Law Reports, Florida Bar Journal, Florida League of Cities, Florida Municipal Record, Florida Trend, The Florida Voter, Human Events, International City Managers Association, The Kiwanis Magazine, Law and Order, Nation's Cities, Opinions of the Attorney General of Florida, Police Chief*

[a]A limited number of other listings have been omitted due to the fact that they could not be found in any of the general or specialized libraries throughout the state.

**Appendix C
General Questionnaire**

A. Personal Information (Place the appropriate number in the space to the left of the question)

_____ 1-2. Title of Occupation

        1. Doctor   6. Law Enforcement Officer
        2. Attorney   7. Bookstore Operator
        3. Judge   8. Moviehouse Operator
        4. Clergy Member 9. School Board Member
        5. School Teacher 10. Lawmaker (legislator, county com-
                              missioner, city or town chairperson)

_____ 3. How Long Have You Held This Position?

        1. Less Than One Year
        2. 1-5 Years
        3. 6 or More Years

_____ 4. How Old Are You?

        1. Below 30 Years
        2. 31-40
        3. 41-50
        4. 51-60
        5. Over 60

_____ 5. What is the Extent of Your Education? (Please Choose the Most Appropriate Category)

        1. Some High School   5. Some Graduate Work
        2. High School Diploma 6. Masters Degree
        3. Two Years College   7. Law Degree
        4. College Degree   8. Ph.D.

_____ 6. What is Your Religion?

        1. Catholic   3. Protestant
        2. Jewish   4. Other (Please specify)_____

B. Awareness and Perceptions of the United States Supreme Court

7-8. How Many Justices are There on The United States Supreme Court?_____

9-10. What is the Name of the Chief Justice of the United States Supreme Court?_____

11. Please List the Names of the The Other Justices
_____

_____

_____ 12.   Do You Feel That the United States Supreme Court is an Important
             Part of Our National Government? (Place the appropriate number
             in the space to the left of the question)

             1. Yes   2. No   3. Unsure

_____ 13.   Do the Decisions of the United States Supreme Court Affect
             Your Personal Life (Your Family and Freedom)?

             1. Yes   2. No   3. Unsure

_____ 14.   Do the Decisions of the United States Supreme Court Affect
             Your Work?

             1. Yes   2. No   3. Unsure

_____ 15.   Do You Feel That it is Important to be Aware of Decisions of
             the United States Supreme Court?

             1. Yes   2. No   3. Unsure

       Has the United States Supreme Court Made a Decision in any of the
       Following Areas in the Past 20 Years? (Yes=1, No=2, Unsure=3)

_____ 16.   Flood Damage   _____ 28.   Lord's Prayer in School

_____ 17.   Right to Council   _____ 29.   Drunk Driving

_____ 18.   Obscene Movies   _____ 30.   Smoking

_____ 19.   Juvenile Rights   _____ 31.   Bible Reading in the School

_____ 20.   Abortions   _____ 32.   Police Lineups

_____ 21.   Drug Offenses   _____ 33.   Reapportionment

_____ 22.   Wiretapping   _____ 34.   Taxing Religious Organizations

_____ 23.   Stop and Frisk   _____ 35.   Dissemination of Birth Control
                                                     Information
_____ 24.   Fire Control   _____ 36.   Double Jeopardy

_____ 25.   Vagrancy   _____ 37.   State Aid to Parochial Schools

_____ 26.   Trial by Jury   _____ 38.   Right to Remain Silent

_____ 27.   Death Penalty   _____ 39.   Obscene Books

C. General Questions on Communication

From Which Sources Do You <u>Usually</u> Obtain <u>Reliable</u> Information About Decisions of the United States Supreme Court? (Yes=1, No=2)

_____ 40. Television or Radio

_____ 41. Newspaper

_____ 42. General Periodicals (Time, Newsweek, etc.)

_____ 43. Specialized Memoranda, Bulletins or Newsletters

_____ 44. Specialized Magazines or Journals

_____ 45. Reading the Opinion Itself

_____ 46. Other. Please Specify_____

From Which Sources Do You <u>Usually</u> Obtain <u>Reliable</u> Information About Decisions of the United States Supreme Court? (Yes=1, No=2)

_____ 47. A Co-Worker

_____ 48. A Boss or Superior

_____ 49. A Subordinate

_____ 50. A Member of A District Attorney's Office

_____ 51. A Member of A Public Defender's Office

_____ 52. Member of the Florida Attorney General's Office

_____ 53. F.B.I. Agent

_____ 54. Conferences and/or Training Sessions. Please Specify_____

        _____

_____ 55. A Friend Not Included Above. Please Specify_____

        _____

_____ 56. Local Judge

_____ 57. Other, Please Specify_____

By What Means Do You <u>Prefer</u> to Obtain Information About Decisions of the United States Supreme Court? (Please Rank in Order of Preference, 1-4)

_____ 58. Written Materials (Newspapers, Reporters, Magazines and the Like)

_____ 59. Electronic Media (Radio and Television)

_____ 60. Lecturer or Speaker

_____ 61. Informal Conversation

What Specific Literature Do You Read <u>At Work</u> Which Contains Information About United States Supreme Court Decisions? (Magazines, Journals, Court Reports, Newsletters, etc.) (Please List All Sources)

_____

_____

What Specific Literature Do You Read <u>At Home</u> Which Contains Information About United States Supreme Court Decisions? (Please List <u>ALL</u> Sources)

_____

_____

_____ 62. Have you Attended Any Conferences, Meetings, Schools or the Like, Which Have Discussed Recent United States Supreme Court Decisions?

1. Yes   2. No   3. Unsure

If Yes, Please List.

_____

_____

_____ 63. Do You Feel That the Communication of Supreme Court Decisions to Your Occupational Group Needs to be Improved?

1. Yes   2. No   3. Unsure

If Yes, How Would You Suggest Improving Them?

_____

_____

_____

Appendix D
Specialized Questionnaires

D. Specialized Area of Inquiry for School Teachers

_____ 64. Please Circle the Type of Organization With Which You Are
          Affiliated. (Circle One)

          1. Public   2. Private Religious   3. Private Non-Sectarian

_____ 65. Please Indicate the Grade Which You Teach (Circle One)

          1. Elementary (1-6)   3. High School (10-12)

          2. Junior High (7-9)

_____ 66. Are You Aware of Supreme Court Decisions Which Deal With
          Financial Aid to Parochial Schools? (Circle One)

          1. Yes   2. No   3. Unsure

_____ 67. If Yes, By What Means Did You Receive the Best Information
          About These Decisions? (Circle One)

          1. Written Materials (Newspapers, Reports, Magazines, etc.)

          2. Electronic Media (Radio and Television)

          3. Lecturer or Speaker

          4. Informal Conversation

_____ 68. Are You Aware of Supreme Court Decisions Dealing With Prayers
          in Public Schools? (Circle One)

          1. Yes   2. No   3. Unsure

_____ 69. If Yes, By What Means Did You Receive the Best Information About
          These Decisions? (Circle One)

          1. Written Materials (Newspapers, Reports, Magazines, etc.)

          2. Electronic Media (Radio and Television)

          3. Lecturer or Speaker

          4. Informal Conversation

_____ 70-72. If Yes, What Do These Decisions Require of School Board Members?

          _____

          _____

_____ 73. Are School Teachers Permitted to Write a Prayer for Morning
          Exercises? (Circle One)

          1. Yes   2. No   3. Unsure

_____ 74. Do School Teachers Have the Right to Allow Bible Reading
          During Morning Exercises? (Circle One)

          1. Yes   2. No   3. Unsure

_____ 75. Do Lawmakers Have the Right to Finance School Systems Using
          A Property Tax Scheme Which Ultimately Allows One District to
          Spend $356 per Pupil and Another to Spend $594 per Pupil?
          (Circle One)

          1. Yes   2. No   3. Unsure

_____ 76. Do School Teachers Have the Right to Allow the Recitation of
          the Lord's Prayer in Public Schools? (Circle One)

          1. Yes   2. No   3. Unsure

_____ 77. Does the Constitution Allow Law Enforcement Officers to Stop
          and Frisk a Suspicious-Looking Person? (Circle One)

          1. Yes   2. No   3. Unsure

_____ 78. Is it Constitutionally Permissible for a State to Prohibit
          Persons From Voting for the President or Vice President Until
          They Have Resided Within the State for Six Months?

          1. Yes   2. No   3. Unsure

From Where Are You Able to Obtain a Copy or Summary of United States
Supreme Court Decisions? (Please List ALL Possible Places)

_____

_____

_____

D. Specialized Area of Inquiry for Judges

_____ 64. Please Circle the Profession in Which You are Employed
           (Circle One)

           1. Trial Judge   2. Appellate Judge

_____ 65. Please Indicate the Size of the City in Which You Work
           (Circle One)

           1. Under 5,000   3. 25,001 - 100,000

           2. 5,001 - 25,000   4. Over 100,000

_____ 66. Are You Aware of the Recent United States Supreme Court Decision
           (Williams v. Florida) Which Deals With the Size of the Jury
           in Criminal Prosecutions? (Circle One)

           1. Yes   2. No   3. Unsure

_____ 67. If Yes, By What Means Did You Receive the Best Information
           About Williams?

           1. Written Materials (Newspapers, Magazines, Reporters, etc.)

           2. Electronic Media (Radio and Television)

           3. Lecturer or Speaker

           4. Informal Conversation

_____ 68. Are You Aware of the Recent United States Supreme Court Decision
           (Argersinger v. Hamlin) Dealing With a Defendant's Right to
           Obtain an Appointed Attorney, Even Though Charged With Only
           a Minor Infraction of the Law? (Circle One)

           1. Yes   2. No   3. Unsure

_____ 69. If Yes, By What Means Did you Receive the Best Information About
           Argersinger? (Circle One)

           1. Written Materials (Newspapers, Reporters, Magazines, etc.)

           2. Electronic Media (Radio and Television)

           3. Lecturer or Speaker

           4. Informal Conversations

_____ 70-72. If Yes, What Does the <u>Argersinger</u> Decision Require of Judges?

_____

_____

_____

_____ 73. Do Juveniles Have the Right to Remain Silent and to Have an
Attorney Present During a Hearing?

1. Yes   2. No   3. Unsure

_____ 74. A Statute Which Allows the Judge or Jury to Use Discretion in
Imposing Either the Death Penalty or Life Imprisonment is
Constitutional. (Circle One)

1. Yes   2. No   3. Unsure

_____ 75. Once a Defendant Has Been Convicted of Violating a City Ordinance,
Can He Be Convicted of Violating a Similar State Statute Using
the Same Evidence? (Circle One)

1. Yes   2. No   3. Unsure

_____ 76. Can a Statement, Inadmissable as Part of the Prosecution's Case
Under <u>Miranda</u>, Nevertheless Be Used to Impeach a Defendant's
Credibility? (Circle One)

1. Yes   2. No   3. Unsure

_____ 77. Does the Person Accused of a Crime Have the Right to Have an
Attorney Present During a Lineup if it is a Critical Stage in
the Process? (Circle One)

1. Yes   2. No   3. Unsure

_____ 78. Is It Constitutionally Permissible For a State to Prohibit
Persons from Voting for the President or Vice President Until
They Have Resided Within The State for Six Months? (Circle One)

1. Yes   2. No   3. Unsure

From Where Are You Able to Obtain a Copy of a United States
Supreme Court Decision? (Please List <u>All</u> Possible Places)

_____

_____

_____

D. Specialized Area of Inquiry for <u>Law Enforcement Officers</u>

_____ 64. Please Indicate the Type of Position in Which You Are Employed

        1. City Police Chief   5. County Captain or Lieutenant

        2. City Captain or   6. County Deputy or Sergeant
            Lieutenant
                                      7. State Police Office
        3. City Police Patrolman   (Sergeant or Above)

        4. County Sheriff   8. State Trooper (I or II) or
                                          Corporal

_____ 65. Please Indicate the Size of the City in Which You Work

        1. Under 5,000   3. 25,001 - 100,000

        2. 5,001 - 25,000   4. Over 100,000

_____ 66. Are You Aware of the Recent Supreme Court Decision Which Held
           That Once a Legal Arrest Has Been Made, Any Contraband Seized
           May Be Admitted As Evidence in a Court of Law?

        1. Yes   2. No   3. Unsure

_____ 67. If Yes, By What Means Did You Receive the Best Information
           About the Decision (Choose One)

        1. Written Materials (Newspapers, Reporters, Magazines, etc.)

        2. Electronic Media (Radio and Television)

        3. Lecturer or Speaker

        4. Informal Conversation

_____ 68. Are You Aware of Any Recent United States Supreme Court Decisions
           Dealing With Vagrancy Ordinances?

        1. Yes   2. No   3. Unsure

_____ 69. If Yes, By What Means Did You Receive the <u>Best</u> Information
           About Them? (Choose One)

        1. Written Materials (Newspapers, Reports, Magazines, etc.)

        2. Electronic Media (Radio and Television)

        3. Lecturer or Speaker

        4. Informal Conversation

_____ 70-72.   If Yes, What Has the United States Supreme Court Generally
               Decided About Vagrancy Ordinances?

               _____

               _____

_____ 73.   Do Juveniles Have the Right to Remain Silent And To Have An
            Attorney Present During a Hearing?

            1. Yes   2. No   3. Unsure

_____ 74.   Is Pumping a Persons Stomach to Retrieve as Evidence, Narcotic
            Pills Which Have Recently Been Swallowed, Constitutionally
            Permissable?

            1. Yes   2. No   3. Unsure

_____ 75.   Is It Constitutionally Permissable to Take a Blood Sample From
            a Person to Determine His Sobriety?

            1. Yes   2. No   3. Unsure

_____ 76.   Does A Person Accused of a Crime Have the Right to Have an
            Attorney Present During a Lineup if it is a Critical Stage in
            the Process?

            1. Yes   2. No   3. Unsure

_____ 77.   Does the Constitution Allow a Law Enforcement Officer to Stop
            and Frisk a Suspicious-Looking Person?

            1. Yes   2. No   3. Unsure

_____ 78.   Is it Constitutionally Permissible For a State to Prohibit
            Persons From Voting for the President or Vice President Until
            They Have Resided Within the State for Six Months?

            1. Yes   2. No   3. Unsure

            From Where Are You Able to Obtain a Copy or Summary of United
            States Supreme Court Decisions? (Please List ALL Possible
            Places)

            _____

            _____

            _____

D. Specialized Area of Inquiry for <u>Attorneys</u>

_____ 64. Please Circle the Type of Profession in Which You Are Employed.

1. State Attorney   4. Assistant Public Defender

2. Assistant State Attorney   5. Private Attorney

3. Public Defender

_____ 65. Please Indicate the Size of the City in Which You Work

1. Under 5,000   3. 25,001 - 100,000

2. 5,001 - 25,000   4. Over 100,000

_____ 66. Are You Aware of the Recent Supreme Court Decision Which Held
That Once A Legal Arrest Has Been Made, Any Contraband Seized
May Be Admitted as Evidence in a Court of Law (<u>Gustafson</u> v.
<u>Florida</u>)? (Circle One)

1. Yes   2. No   3. Unsure

_____ 67. If Yes, By What Means Did You Receive the Best Information About
This Decision? (Circle One)

1. Written Materials (Newspapers, Reports, Magazines, etc.)

2. Electronic Media (Radio and Television)

3. Lecturer or Speaker

4. Informal Conversations

_____ 68. Are You Aware of the Recent Supreme Court Decision (<u>Argersinger</u>
v. <u>Hamlin</u>) Dealing With a Defendant's Right to Obtain an
Appointed Attorney, Even Though Charged With Only a Minor
Infraction of the Law? (Circle One)

1. Yes   2. No   3. Unsure

_____ 69. If Yes, By What Means Did You Receive the Best Information About
<u>Argersinger</u>? (Circle One)

1. Written Materials (Newspapers, Reports, Magazines, etc.)

2. Electronic Media (Radio and Television)

3. Lecturer or Speaker

4. Informal Conversations

_____ 70-72. If Yes, What Does The Decision Require of Attorneys?

_____

_____

_____ 73. Does A Defendant Always Have the Right to a Jury Trial in Instances Where He May Receive a Sentence of Two Years Imprisonment? (Circle One)

1. Yes   2. No   3. Unsure

_____ 74. A Statute Which Allows the Judge to Use Discretion in Imposing Either the Death Penalty or Life Imprisonment is Constitutional? (Circle One)

1. Yes   2. No   3. Unsure

_____ 75. Once a Defendant Has Been Convicted of Violating a City Ordinance, Can He Be Convicted of Violating a Similar State Statute Using the Same Evidence? (Circle One)

1. Yes   2. No   3. Unsure

_____ 76. Can a Statement, Inadmissable as Part of a Prosecutor's Case, Nevertheless Be Used to Impeach a Defendant's Credibility? (Circle One)

1. Yes   2. No   3. Unsure

_____ 77. Does a Person Accused of a Crime, Have the Right to Have an Attorney Present During a Lineup? (Circle One)

1. Yes   2. No   3. Unsure

_____ 78. Is it Constitutionally Permissible for a State to Prohibit Persons From Voting for the President or Vice President Until They Have Resided Within the State for Six Months? (Circle One)

1. Yes   2. No   3. Unsure

From Where Are You Able to Obtain a Copy of a United States Supreme Court Decision? (Please List ALL Possible Places)

_____

_____

_____

D. Specialized Area of Inquiry for <u>Lawmakers</u>

_____ 64. Please Circle the Type of Position in Which You Are Employed.
           (Circle One)

           1. City Mayor   4. Cty. Commission-Member

           2. City Councilperson   5. Chairperson, St. Legis.
                                                 Comm.
           3. County Commission Chairperson
                                             6. State Legislator

_____ 65. Please Indicate the Size of the City in Which You Work.
           (Circle One)

           1. Under 5,000   3. 25,001 - 100,000

           2. 5,001 - 25,000   4. Over 100,000

_____ 66. Are You Aware of Some of the Recent United States Supreme Court
           Decisions Dealing With Vagrancy Ordinances? (Circle One)

           1. Yes   2. No   3. Unsure

_____ 67. If Yes, By What Means Did You Receive the <u>Best</u> Information
           About Them? (Circle One)

           1. Written Materials (Newspapers, Reports, Magazines, etc.)

           2. Electronic Media (Radio and Television)

           3. Lecturer or Speaker

           4. Informal Conversation

_____ 68. Are You Aware of the United States Supreme Court Decisions
           Dealing With Reapportionment? (Circle One)

           1. Written Materials (Newspapers, Reports, Magazines, etc.)

           2. Electronic Media (Radio and Television)

           3. Lecturer or Speaker

           4. Informal Conversation

_____ 70-72. If Yes, What Do These Decisions Require of Lawmakers?

           _____

           _____

           _____

_____ 73. Do Lawmakers Have the Right to Censor Obscene Movies?
          (Circle One)

          1. Yes   2. No   3. Unsure

_____ 74. Do Lawmakers Have the Right to Allow the Recitation of the
          Lord's Prayer in Public Schools? (Circle One)

          1. Yes   2. No   3. Unsure

_____ 75. Do Lawmakers Have the Right to Prohibit Abortions During the
          First Three Months of Pregnancy? (Circle One)

          1. Yes   2. No   3. Unsure

_____ 76. Do Lawmakers Have the Right to Finance School Systems Using
          a Property Tax Scheme Which Ultimately Allows One District to
          Spend $356 per Pupil and Another to Spend $594 per Pupil?
          (Circle One)

          1. Yes   2. No   3. Unsure

_____ 77. A Statute Which Allows the Judge or Jury to Use Discretion in
          Imposing Either the Death Penalty or Life Imprisonment is
          Constitutional. (Circle One)

          1. Yes   2. No   3. Unsure

_____ 78. Is it Constitutionally Permissible for a State to Prohibit
          Persons From Voting for the President or Vice President Until
          They Have Resided Within the State for Six Months? (Circle One)

          1. Yes   2. No   3. Unsure

          From Where Are You Able to Obtain a Copy of a United States
          Supreme Court Decision? (Please List ALL Possible Places)

          _____

          _____

          _____

D. Specialized Area of Inquiry for <u>School Board Members</u>

_____ 64. Please Circle the Type of Organization With Which You Are
           Affiliated. (Circle One)

           1. City   2. County   3. State

_____ 65. Please Indicate the Size of the City in Which You Work. (Circle One)

           1. Under 5,000   3. 25,001 - 100,000

           2. 5,001 - 25,000   4. Over 100,000

_____ 66. Are You Aware of Supreme Court Decisions Which Deal With Financial
           Aid to Parochial Schools? (Circle One)

           1. Yes   2. No   3. Unsure

_____ 67. If Yes, By What Means Did You Receive the <u>Best</u> Information
           About These Decisions? (Circle One)

           1. Written Materials (Newspapers, Reports, Magazines, etc.)

           2. Electronic Media (Radio and Television)

           3. Lecturer or Speaker

           4. Informal Conversation

_____ 68. Are You Aware of Supreme Court Decisions Dealing With Prayers
           in Public Schools? (Circle One)

           1. Yes   2. No   3. Unsure

_____ 69. If Yes, By What Means Did You Receive the <u>Best</u> Information About
           These Decisions? (Circle One)

           1. Written Materials (Newspapers, Reports, Magazines, etc.)

           2. Electronic Media (Radio and Television)

           3. Lecturer or Speaker

           4. Informal Conversation

_____ 70-72. If Yes, What Do These Decisions Require of School Board Members?

           _____

           _____

_____ 73. Are Lawmakers permitted to Write a Prayer for Morning Exercises? (Circle One)

1. Yes   2. No   3. Unsure

_____ 74. Do Lawmakers Have the Right to Allow Bible Reading During Morning Exercises? (Circle One)

1. Yes   2. No   3. Unsure

_____ 75. Do Lawmakers Have the Right to Finance School Systems Using a Property Tax Scheme Which Ultimately Allows One District to Spend $356 per Pupil and Another to Spend $594 per Pupil? (Circle One)

1. Yes   2. No   3. Unsure

_____ 76. Do Lawmakers Have the Right to Allow the Recitation of the Lord's Prayer in Public Schools? (Circle One)

1. Yes   2. No   3. Unsure

_____ 77. Does the Constitution Allow a Law Enforcement Officer to Stop and Frisk a Suspicious-Looking Person? (Circle One)

1. Yes   2. No   3. Unsure

_____ 78. Is it Constitutionally Permissible for a State to Prohibit Persons From Voting for the President or Vice President Until They Have Resided Within the State for Six Months? (Circle One)

1. Yes   2. No   3. Unsure

From Where Are You Able to Obtain a Copy or Summary of United States Supreme Court Decisions? (Please List ALL Possible Places)

_____

_____

_____

D. Specialized Area of Inquiry for <u>Book Store and Movie House Operators</u>

____ 64. Please Circle the Type of Management With Which You Are
            Connected.

    1. Movie Theater   2. Non-Profit Book Store   3. Profit Book
                                                            Store

____ 65. Please Indicate the Size of the City in Which You Work.
            (Circle One)

    1. Under 5,000   3. 25,001 - 100,000

    2. 5,001 - 25,000   4. Over 100,000

____ 66. Are You Aware of the Recent Supreme Court Decisions Dealing
            With the Dissemination of Obscene Literature? (Circle One)

    1. Yes   2. No   3. Unsure

____ 67. If Yes, By What Means Did You Receive the <u>Best</u> Information
            About It? (Circle One)

    1. Written Materials (Newspapers, Reports, Magazines, etc.)

    2. Electronic Media (Radio and Television)

    3. Lecturer or Speaker

    4. Informal Conversation

____ 68. Are You Aware of the Recent Supreme Court Decision Dealing With
            Obscene Movies? (Circle One)

    1. Yes   2. No   3. Unsure

____ 69. If Yes, By What Means Did You Receive the <u>Best</u> Information About
            the Decision? (Circle One)

    1. Written Materials (Newspapers, Reports, Magazines, etc.)

    2. Electronic Media (Radio and Television)

    3. Lecturer or Speaker

    4. Informal Conversation

_____ 70-72.   If Yes, What Does the Decision Require of Movie Theater
               Operators?

               _____

               _____

_____ 73.   What Geographic Area is Utilized to Determine "Contemporary
            Community Standards"?   (Circle One)

            1. Local   2. National   3. Unsure

_____ 74.   Have These Decisions Hurt Your Business Economically? (Circle One)

            1. Yes   2. No   3. Unsure

_____ 75.   Have These Recent Decisions Hurt Your Moral Standing in the
            Community in Which you Work?   (Circle One)

            1. Yes   2. No   3. Unsure

_____ 76.   Do You Agree That the Recent Decisions Should Have Been Decided
            As They Were?   (Circle One)

            1. Yes   2. No   3. Unsure

_____ 77.   Have These Recent Decisions Helped You in Any Way?   (Circle One)

            1. Yes   2. No   3. Unsure

            If So, How?_____

            _____

_____ 70.   Is it Constitutionally Permissible For a State to Prohibit Persons
            From Voting for the President or Vice President Until They
            Have Resided Within the State for Six Months?   (Circle One)

            1. Yes   2. No   3. Unsure

            From Where Are You Able to Obtain a Copy or Summary of United
            States Supreme Court Decisions?   (Please List ALL Possible Places)

            _____

            _____

            _____

D. Specialized Area of Inquiry for <u>Doctors</u>

_____ 64. Please Indicate Your Specialization.

_____   _____

_____ 65. Please Indicate the Size of the City in Which You Work.
           (Circle One)

           1. Under 5,000   3. 25,001 - 100,000

           2. 5,001 - 25,000   4. Over 100,000

_____ 66. Are You Aware of the Supreme Court Decision Which Dealt With
           the Dissemination of Birth Control Information? (Circle One)

           1. Yes   2. No   3. Unsure

_____ 67. If Yes, By What Means Did You Receive the <u>Best</u> Information
           About the Decision? (Circle One)

           1. Written Materials (Newspapers, Reports, Magazines, etc.)

           2. Electronic Media (Radio and Television)

           3. Lecturer or Speaker

           4. Informal Conversation

_____ 68. Are You Aware of the Recent United States Supreme Court Decisions
           Dealing With Abortion? (Circle One)

           1. Yes   2. No   3. Unsure

_____ 69. If Yes, By What Means Did You Receive the <u>Best</u> Information About
           Them? (Circle One)

           1. Written Materials (Newspapers, Reports, Magazines, etc.)

           2. Electronic Media (Radio and Television)

           3. Lecturer or Speaker

           4. Informal Conversation

_____ 70-72. If Yes, What Has the United States Supreme Court Generally
              Decided About the Performance of Abortions?

           _____

           _____

_____ 73. Do You Favor the Abortion Decisions? (Circle One)

    1. Yes   2. No   3. Unsure

_____ 74. Is Pumping a Person's Stomach to Retrieve as Evidence, Narcotic
      Pills Which Have Recently Been Swallowed, Constitutionally
      Permissible   (Circle One)

    1. Yes   2. No   3. Unsure

_____ 75. Is it Constitutionally Permissible to Take a Blood Sample
      From a Person to Determine His Sobriety? (Circle One)

    1. Yes   2. No   3. Unsure

_____ 76. Is it Constitutionally Permissible Without a Judicial Warrant,
      to Administer Blood Transfusions to Save a Child's Life Despite
      Parental Objections? (Circle One)

    1. Yes   2. No   3. Unsure

_____ 77. Does the Constitution Allow a Law Enforcement Officer to Stop
      and Frisk a Suspicious-Looking Person? (Circle One)

    1. Yes   2. No   3. Unsure

_____ 78. Is it Constitutionally Permissible For a State to Prohibit
      Persons From Voting for the President or Vice President Until
      They Have Resided Within the State for Six Months? (Circle One)

    1. Yes   2. No   3. Unsure

      From Where Are You Able to Obtain a Copy or Summary of United
      States Supreme Court Decisions? (Please List ALL Possible Places)

      _____

      _____

      _____

D. Specialized Area of Inquiry for <u>Clergymen</u>

_____ 64. Please Indicate Your Occupation.

        1. Catholic Priest

        2. Jewish Rabbi

        3. Protestant Minister

        4. Other (Specify)_____

_____ 65. Please Indicate the Size of the City in Which You Work.
           (Circle One)

        1. Under 5,000   3. 25,001 - 100,000

        2. 5,001 - 25,000   4. Over 100,000

_____ 66. Are You Aware of the Supreme Court Decision Which Dealt With
           the Dissemination of Birth Control Information?(Circle One)

        1. Yes   2. No   3. Unsure

_____ 67. If Yes, By What Means Did You Receive the <u>Best</u> Information
           About the Decision? (Circle One)

        1. Written Materials (Newspapers, Reports, Magazines, etc.)

        2. Electronic Media (Radio and Television)

        3. Lecturer or Speaker

        4. Informal Conversation

_____ 68. Are You Aware of the Recent United States Supreme Court Decisions
           Dealing With Abortion? (Circle One)

        1. Yes   2. No   3. Unsure

_____ 69. If Yes, By What Means Did You Receive the <u>Best</u> Information
           About Them? (Circle One)

         1. Written Materials (Newspapers, Reports, Magazines, etc.)

        2. Electronic Media (Radio and Television)

        3. Lecturer or Speaker

        4. Informal Conversation

_____ 70-72. If Yes, What Has the United States Supreme Court Generally
              Decided About the Performance of Abortions?

       _____

       _____

       _____

_____ 73. Do You Favor the Abortion Decisions? (Circle One)

           1. Yes   2. No   3. Unsure

_____ 74. Are Lawmakers Permitted to Write a Prayer for Morning Exercises?
           (Circle One)

           1. Yes   2. No   3. Unsure

_____ 75. Do Lawmakers Have the Right to Allow Bible Reading During Morning
           Exercises? (Circle One)

           1. Yes   2. No   3. Unsure

_____ 76. Do Lawmakers Have the Right to Finance School Systems Using a
           Property Tax Scheme Which Ultimately Allows One District to
           Spend $356 per Pupil and Another to Spend $594 per Pupil?
           (Circle One)

           1. Yes   2. No   3. Unsure

_____ 77. Do Lawmakers Have the Right to Allow the Recitation of the Lord's
           Prayer in Public Schools? (Circle One)

           1. Yes   2. No   3. Unsure

_____ 78. Is it Constitutionally Permissible for a State to Prohibit
           Persons From Voting for the President or Vice President Until
           They Have Resided Within the State for Six Months? (Circle One)

           1. Yes   2. No   3. Unsure

           From Where Are You Able to Obtain a Copy or Summary of United
           States Supreme Court Decisions? (Please List ALL Possible
           Places)

       _____

       _____

       _____

Index

143

About the Author

Larry C. Berkson received the Ph.D. in political science from the University of Wisconsin in 1973. He is currently on leave from the department of political science, University of Florida, Gainesville, as a visiting fellow at the American Judicature Society. There he is principal investigator for an LEAA funded project studying court unification. He is coauthor of *Managing the State Courts* and author of *The Concept of Cruel and Unusual Punishment.* Professor Berkson is also the author of numerous articles on judicial administration, court management and constitutional law. During the summer of 1975, he received the Board of Regents' Faculty Internship in Criminal Justice Grant through LEAA to serve as a deputy clerk in the Eighth Judicial Circuit, Florida. The following spring he was a judicial fellow finalist at the U.S. Supreme Court.

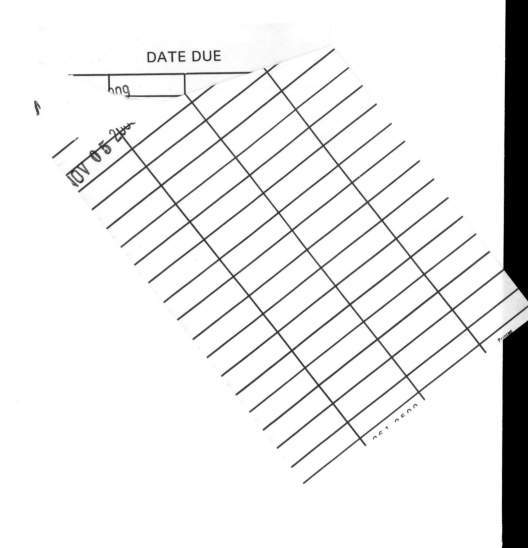

DATE DUE

NOV 05 2001